D0925820

WITHDRAWN
UTSA LIBRARIES

The 12 Laws of Urban School Leadership

A Principal's Guide for Initiating Effective Change

Sean B. Yisrael

ROWMAN & LITTLEFIELD EDUCATION
A division of
ROWMAN & LITTLEFIELD PUBLISHERS, INC.
Lanham • New York • Toronto • Plymouth, UK

Published by Rowman & Littlefield Education
A division of Rowman & Littlefield Publishers, Inc.
A wholly owned subsidiary of The Rowman & Littlefield Publishing Group, Inc.
4501 Forbes Boulevard, Suite 200, Lanham, Maryland 20706
www.rowman.com

10 Thornbury Road, Plymouth PL6 7PP, United Kingdom

Copyright © 2012 by Sean B. Yisrael

All rights reserved. No part of this book may be reproduced in any form or by any
electronic or mechanical means, including information storage and retrieval systems,
without written permission from the publisher, except by a reviewer who may quote
passages in a review.

British Library Cataloguing in Publication Information Available

Library of Congress Cataloging-in-Publication Data

Yisrael, Sean B.
The 12 laws of urban school leaderhip : a principal's guide for initiating effective change / Sean B.
Yisrael.
p. cm.
Includes bibliographical references.
ISBN 978-1-61048-824-2 (cloth : alk. paper) -- ISBN 978-1-61048-825-9 (pbk. : alk. paper) -- ISBN
978-1-61048-826-6 (electronic)
1. Urban schools--United States--Administration. 2. School improvement programs--United States. I.
Title. II. Title: Twelve laws of urban school leadership.
LC5131.Y57 2012
370.9173'20973--dc23
2012002373

♾™   The paper used in this publication meets the minimum requirements of American
National Standard for Information Sciences Permanence of Paper for Printed Library
Materials, ANSI/NISO Z39.48-1992.

Printed in the United States of America

Library
University of Texas
at San Antonio

Contents

Foreword

This book is essential reading that will challenge current and aspiring urban school leaders. Dr. Yisrael urges school leaders to be reflective practitioners. His work suggests that transformation is required from school leaders in urban settings, in order to challenge school policies and practices that lead to academic disparities for disenfranchised students.

His narratives give the reader a clear description of the day-to-day realities encountered by urban school leaders as they grapple to initiate change in their respective buildings. His work will make individuals question their philosophy, beliefs, and core values. He emphasizes that urban leadership is more than being able to "recite" philosophical jargon.

He challenges urban school leaders to commit to engaging the community in meaningful conversations in an effort to enhance the school environment. Dr. Yisrael indicates that school leaders ought to ensure the delivery of high-quality instruction founded on research-based practices and ongoing assessment and progress monitoring.

Most important, Dr. Yisrael challenges school leaders to avoid making decisions based on pressure from groups or individuals who hold political capital and influence. From start to finish he captivates the reader with his uncompromising ability to challenge the status quo head on while confronting educative practices that render minimal results. His book starts off with the most important individual, the school leader.

Dr. Yisrael's book is about laws to be used as a guide for school leaders to hold themselves and their colleagues accountable. Law 1, *Guard Your Most Sacred Assets*, is vitally important and chapter 1 contains invaluable advice that should guide every school leader. It is premised on taking care of oneself via dieting, exercising, subscribing to educational publications, attending professional workshops, and spending quality time with family and loved ones.

As Dr. Yisrael explains it, leaders will falter unless they place themselves on the priority list. Law 2, *Learn the Culture of the School and Community*, is indispensable for the survival of the urban school leader. In chapter 2 Dr. Yisrael discusses how school leadership is heavily entangled in politics. He spends a significant amount of time strongly recommending that leaders get well acquainted with the community, the school district, and present and past achievements of the community, and understand thoroughly that no two districts are alike. He posits that much is expected from urban school principals in spite of drastic budget cuts and diminished student enrollment. He suggests that the leader start with a close examination of past data, which will drive instructional methods.

Law 3 is *Become a Supreme Pragmatist*, and chapter 3 provides practical suggestions for judging personnel based on results, not lip service. Dr. Yisrael suggests that individuals often pretend to be contributors to school leadership. However, their egotistical motives are soon revealed as the school year progresses. Dr. Yisrael again reiterates the importance of utilizing data to make informed decisions as it pertains to student achievement.

In chapter 12 Dr. Yisrael discusses the final law, *Creating a Strategic Plan for Improving Student Discipline and Staff Morale.* This is not only important in urban school settings, but also for public schools as a whole. Due to the increased demands on education professionals to produce high levels of student achievement with limited or no resources, most public schools have staff members who are overworked, drained, and literally burned out. When this happens, principals have an extremely hard time trying to move student achievement forward. Dr. Yisrael not only discusses why a plan of action is needed for these vital areas, but he also instructs principals on how to create such a plan.

It is not my intention to outline the entire book. Conversely, I wanted to merely entice the reader with short snapshots of the excellent work presented by Dr. Yisrael. This book is indeed needed and should be an essential text for those working in the trenches, specifically in the urban school environment. School leaders working in this setting can utilize the book to spark the difficult conversations that may go unsaid. This book is essential, and I highly recommend that you indulge yourself with a comfortable place to sit, because this book is difficult to put down.

Carlos L. Blair, EdD
High School Principal

Preface

You Want to Become a Principal in an Urban School District?

THE ORIGIN OF THE 12 LAWS

My inspiration for writing this book happened accidentally. A few years ago, I was working on a qualitative case study on a leadership topic not directly related to the topics discussed in this book. The study involved 60 urban school principals who had success at reforming their respective schools. In order to work my hypothesis, I conducted taped interviews, transcribed the notes from such interviews, and triangulated the data.

The administrators who participated in the study were very forthright with answering my pre-written questions. The conversations were so candid, entertaining, and informative that we would often venture into other topics related to urban/inner-city education and school leadership in general. Many of the participants told vivid stories about their experiences in urban school administration and what they did to overcome obstacles.

The information they shared dealt with the realities of the position. In most colleges and universities around the country, school reform is often discussed from a utopian perspective, which causes the discourse to be disconnected from what urban principals really need to know in order to be successful. The administrators in the study told the ugly truth about all aspects of their roles as urban school principals, which not only connected to the true nature of being a principal in an urban school district, but also served as a roadmap for successful reforms—which I found to be rather refreshing. The stories they told still resonate with me until this day. Even after the study ended, I found myself listening to those taped interviews in an effort to absorb some of the profound knowledge and wisdom those school administrators possessed.

As I studied the taped interviews, several themes began to emerge. Next, I started to categorize the themes and reorganize my notes. The principals not only spoke about implementing key reforms, boosting student achievement, and operating efficiently, but they also spoke of how to survive in the position. Many urban schools do not have solid leadership simply because they can't get one person to stay in the position long enough, or they may have a person who has been in the position too long and needs to step aside.

Some urban school districts have been underperforming for so long that they're now under intense pressure. In some cases they want microwave-like results, and when the principal does not deliver as expected, he/she is removed from the position and replaced by someone else. There are also urban school districts that are stagnant and continue to accept the status quo. They keep principals in positions simply because they've always been there, despite drops in student achievement. The principals who participated in my case study offered their perspective on these and other relevant topics associated with leading an urban/inner-city school. It was out of these conversations that the 12 laws were formed.

PROBLEMS FACING THE URBAN PRINCIPALSHIP

So you want to be a principal in an urban school? Well this is what you will have to look forward to. With any principalship (urban or otherwise) there will be a lot of long hours, under-appreciation, and relatively low pay compared to other professions with comparable education and status. The thing that sets most urban/inner-city school districts apart is that most of them in America are in a serious crisis (especially the larger ones). The majority are plagued by annual shrinking budgets, pressure from high-stakes testing, high employee turnover, increased competition from charter schools, pressure from state and federal mandates, and habitually low student achievement, just to name a few.

Principals in urban districts are faced with the daunting task of providing leadership in school buildings that are usually underfunded, poorly maintained, inadequately staffed, and in a state of perpetual failure. The urban school principal's role becomes even more challenging when having to contend with teachers' unions, parent-teacher organizations, local school decision-making committees, community grassroots organizations, extreme behavioral issues from students, and negative attention from the media.

In affluent school districts, some of the above-mentioned groups generally work in collaboration with local schools, but because of the factors that have negatively impacted urban education (demographic changes within the communities, high unemployment, crime, violence, etc.), these groups have taken a more adversarial stance when it comes to urban schools. Many people have lost faith in urban education (and public education as a whole). They show their discontent with their protest (failing levies and opting for private or charter schools). In the midst of all this sits the urban school principal. Individuals who occupy this position must possess leadership qualities that meet the extreme needs and diverse circumstances of the students, staff, and communities in which the schools are located.

It takes a special kind of leader who can come into an urban school and succeed. Principals who work in this climate will have their every move and decision scrutinized and contested. Their authority will be challenged by their own staff, students, parents, and any average Joe who thinks he knows how to run a school.

To make the job even more difficult, there are individuals who benefit from failing urban schools. There are people working on the outside, and from within, who want to keep the status quo (failure). On the surface, they'll give the appearance of cooperation and concern for the principal and his/her attempts to make improvements, but in reality they're secretly working against any effort of true reform. They'll patiently wait for the opportunity when a principal will make a mistake, or for a situation to exploit.

PRACTICAL PURPOSE OF THIS BOOK

As I mentioned previously, the information I learned when doing the case study had a profound effect on me. The experience prompted me to write this book in order to share what I've learned with other urban school leaders. *The 12 Laws of Urban School Leadership* is designed to give urban school principals intimate knowledge of the issues faced when working in urban school settings, as well as outline practical strategies for handling such issues.

Principals will learn the best methods for conducting their own actions so they will be able to keep their jobs for as long as they want to occupy the position. The 12 laws outlined in this book will serve as a bridge between what most school leaders learn in graduate schools, and what really happens in an urban/inner-city school (especially one with a history of failure).

Most educational leadership programs in graduate schools across America are built on doctrines and philosophies associated with collaboration, teamwork, relationship building, peace making, and community engagement.

These tenets are all good concepts that school leadership candidates should be exposed to, but trying to implement them in most failing urban/inner-city schools is like trying to force a round ball through a square opening.

Many of the theories taught in graduate school leadership programs do not prepare potential principals for the harsh realities of urban schools (especially those in the inner city), nor do they inform candidates about how to navigate through the increasingly politically charged nature of the position. As a result, the position becomes a revolving door, having one unprepared candidate after another. This eventually hurts the urban schools affected, and the people within them.

Most urban/inner-city schools in this country are saturated with gross inefficiency and dysfunction. These characteristics, and others like them, have settled into the fabric of urban schools and have infected the thinking of all stakeholders involved (students, parents, staff, and community). In this condition, attempts at any real change by school leaders will be misinterpreted and met with opposition.

If principals are not careful in dealing with such oppositional forces, these could grow into deadly weeds that will eventually cover and choke the life out of any, and all, efforts for true reform. At their worst and most powerful state, the weeds (oppositional forces) could lead to the termination of the principal.

It's not uncommon to find that most people become resigned and comfortable with their thinking and environmental conditions in the absence of a strong force pressing the need for change. When they have achieved a certain level of comfort, some humans lose their capacity to think outside the box and to come up with new, exciting, and innovative ideas. Unfortunately for urban schools, most of the stakeholders suffer from stagnation.

They have become comfortable with the chaos, low performance, inefficiency, and dysfunction surrounding them. They've become so comfortable with the way things are, and have always been, that they've stopped believing things can be better. Principals are the leaders and should serve as the pressing force for change.

The 12 laws presented in this book should be followed by all school leaders occupying an urban/inner-city school principalship. They offer a no-nonsense, bare-bones approach to school reform. They touch on the realities of the position without an abundance of philosophical fluff. Each particular law is presented with an explanation of why the law is important, followed by a narrative of the actual situation experienced by one of the participants of the case study (the names of the principals, places, schools, and people involved have been changed to protect the identities of the principals who participated in the study). These laws are for principals who want effective change in their schools, and are willing to confront the tough issues in order to get the job done. Things do not have to remain the same in urban schools—they can get better.

The final purpose of this book is to assist urban school principals with getting rid of negative forces that plague urban/inner-city schools. If followed and implemented correctly the 12 laws will serve as a roadmap for success, giving principals the ability to initiate and deal with conflict effectively, while serving as a positive agent for change. Principals will be able to clearly understand which items are most important, and how to implement the change that's needed.

The laws will serve as a guide, helping urban school principals deal with the extreme situations they will experience—bridging the gap between theory and practice. They will learn how to successfully execute the balancing act of improving overall school performance, while dogging the pitfalls that could cause them to lose their jobs. Urban school principals can use these laws as the catalyst for the effective change needed to reform, and in some cases, recreate the learning environment in their schools.

Introduction

The first six chapters of this book deal with a principal's ability to "set a solid foundation." The chapters include setting a solid foundation not only for the school's overall success, but also for the principal's individual success. In the often unpredictable, volatile, and ever-changing world of urban education, principals need to cement their beliefs and ideologies about education.

Urban school principals who don't have a solid foundation find themselves caught up in constructs that have little to do with the educational process, or the growth and development of the school. They find themselves entangled in rumors and innuendos, reacting to the whims of others, jumping on educational fads and fly-by-night schemes, being overly concerned with being liked and accepted by others, and/or disconnected to the events and people that are shaping the school's culture and practices (just to name a few). Principals who are able to set a solid foundation for themselves are best equipped at setting one for their respective schools. When they encounter turbulence from the changes they implement, they will be able to withstand the turbulence without feeling doubtful, unsure, and insecure.

The last six chapters discuss how urban school principals should "move forward." After the foundation has been set, principals can now begin to take their schools to the next level. This means they must concentrate and maximize all of their physical and human resources in the most effective manner possible. They're building on strengths and improving upon weaknesses. They're changing the overall culture of the school by putting the right people in the right places. Items that once were initiatives have become natural parts of the school's functioning.

Urban schools, especially those located in the inner city, serve communities that are some of the most underprivileged in our country. These communities, and their schools, lack the necessary resources and support to function effectively. In order for true education reform to take place, and to improve the overall economic health of this country, an adequate amount of time and energy must be directed toward the betterment of these schools.

The quality of schools plays a major role in the standard of living shared by communities and society as a whole. The first step in improving schools is by starting with the people who will lead them. Urban school principals not only have to serve as the academic leaders, but they must also be able to effectively deal with the tough issues and people that have been affected by years of incompetence, stagnation, and inefficiency. *The 12 Laws of Urban School Leadership* is a step in that direction.

I

Setting a Solid Foundation

Chapter One

Law 1: Guard Your Most Sacred Assets

Being a principal in an urban school district is arguably one of the most challenging, and stressful, school administrative positions one can occupy. Urban school principals have to juggle the needs of the school, students, staff, and the greater community while being under an intense microscope. At any given moment, the principal could be engulfed by a host of issues, situations, and problems from a multitude of angles (students, staff, parents, media, etc.).

Most urban schools have an extremely high population of students who come from families of low socioeconomic status. These students bring to school environmental, psychological, social, and/or emotional issues, making the barriers for successful teaching and learning more difficult. Despite the many barriers to learning and obstacles these students present, urban schools are still held to the same educational outcomes and academic performance standards of schools whose students do not have the same or similar issues, like those attending more affluent, suburban, or provincial schools.

The various student issues, mixed with other common aspects found in most urban schools (low teacher morale, disgruntled parents, probing and antagonizing media, low resources, poorly maintained buildings, etc.), create a very intense environment to work in. If the principal is not careful, he/she can quickly lose sight of his/her purpose and the real reason for leading the school. This intense environment is the reason why urban school principals must hold on to their most sacred assets.

A principal's most sacred assets are his/her mental and physical health, core philosophy and beliefs about education, and the effective use of time. These are the big three. Protecting your three most important assets is the first law you must follow. Failure to follow this law will put you in a position where you will not be beneficial to your loved ones, yourself, or the school you are trying to lead.

YOUR MENTAL AND PHYSICAL HEALTH

The most essential component to your survival as an urban/inner-city school principal is your physical and mental health. You must take good care of yourself. This means getting regular checkups and examinations from your doctor, having a proper diet, exercising regularly, enjoying pleasurable activities outside of work, and spending adequate quality time with your family and loved ones. If you don't take care of yourself, how will you be able to take care of others?

Many principals in urban school districts work an average of 14 to 16 hours per day, usually without taking sufficient time to eat. Some often grab snacks and eat on the run, while others neglect to eat at all. Something as subtle as eating balanced and nutritional meals daily can have a huge impact on an urban school principal's ability to perform the duties of the job over the long haul.

Urban school principals face obstacles on all levels. You must be mentally sharp and physically fit in order to be successful. Your mental and physical health is your greatest asset. Failure to protect your health will result in your becoming burned out, ill, crazy, hard to live with, and/or headed for a premature retirement.

YOUR CORE PHILOSOPHY AND BELIEFS

Your core philosophy, beliefs, and values are non-negotiable. Never sacrifice them for any reason! These ideas represent the heart of who you are as a person, your uniqueness as a school administrator, and reasons why you decided to enter the education profession in the first place. Sacrificing your core beliefs is like doing away with a part of yourself.

Many urban school principals sacrifice their beliefs, which ultimately leads to their demise. They do so when they make critical decisions against their better judgment, or neglect to speak out when they should. They also do this when they let friendships or associations affect their overall judgment—making decisions that have little to do with student achievement, and more to do with succumbing to pressures from groups or individuals who appear to have political capital or some form of influence.

When principals protect their core beliefs and values, they will not be easily moved by the "fly-by-night" fads that seem to come along in education annually. They will not fold under pressure from self-serving groups and/or individuals. Above all, they will be able to make decisions with a clear conscience.

When you make decisions with a clear conscience, you will not have to worry about the outcome of such decisions, or what others are going to think. You will not worry because your decisions will be made from the depth of your strongest convictions about education, and what's good for students and the school. Regardless of the outcome, you will be able to live with the results. This will help you sleep better at night and feel good about yourself as a school leader and a person.

THE EFFECTIVE USE OF TIME

You must use your time in the most efficient manner possible. It is a very precious commodity that should be highly valued and not wasted. Treat your time as if it were gold or silver. Being a principal puts you in great demand. Everyone from central office personnel to alumni will be lobbying for your time. Various individuals will come into the school daily (sometimes unannounced), and request to meet with you. Principals who do not use their time effectively will find themselves literally in meeting after meeting, day in and day out.

Education is the only profession where any Tom, Dick, and Harriett can appear and demand a meeting and become upset if their request isn't granted instantly, regardless of what the principal has planned for that day, what issues are happening at the moment in the school, or how trivial the matter is. Administrators in other professions (e.g., the business sector) are not expected to be as accessible as school principals are.

Many principals say that they have an open-door policy, and that they're willing to meet with anyone at any time to discuss any and all concerns of the school. This sounds good to the ears, but to do so will literally keep principals trapped in the office and out of the trenches where the real action is (in the classrooms and hallways, and tending to other important school business throughout the school). The best way to protect your time is to be organized.

The principal's calendar will fill up quickly. If you're not organized with your time, you will find yourself working inefficiently. You'll be rushing from one place to another, working on things that can wait until later, reacting to every person you encounter, and meeting with people who will not advance your goals for school improvement. In short, you will be wasting time.

Effective principals plan their calendars with their secretaries in advance. You should designate a block of time (two days per week, for example, or an hour or two out of each day) for meetings and appointments, and stick to your schedule no matter what. Do not allow others to disrupt your schedule by popping in unannounced. If you want to take time for such individuals outside of your schedule, then have them walk with you as you move throughout the halls. This will cause your random visitors to keep it brief and to the point. They will be satisfied because you gave them a bit of your time, and you'll be happy because you were able to avoid the confinement of the office.

Finally, there is a ton of work that needs to be done in most urban schools. You must spend the bulk of your time on items that count—meaning items that will improve the school overall. Principals who spend time in insignificant meetings, or who are confined to their office, get less of the important items accomplished.

Confinement to the office will take the principal out of the battlefield and isolate him/her from the realities that are shaping the school. Urban school principals need to be mobile, fluid, and part of the action in order to be successful. The principal's office can be compared to a dead person's coffin. Stay out of the coffin and you will be able to stay alive as a principal.

EXAMPLE

When Mr. Measley took over the principalship of an urban high school, he was ecstatic. He always wanted to be an administrator in an urban high school because that's where he thought he could have the biggest impact, unlike most of his graduate school colleagues who opted to work in affluent schools or in the private sector. Measley wanted to make sure he did a good job, so he put all he had into his work. He served in the position for 10 years.

Over the course of that time, he worked long hours (averaging 14 hours per day), attended every function and school-related event, and even volunteered to serve on several committees and work with groups within the community. He worked so hard that he would rarely sit down to eat his lunch. He ate on the go, or he grabbed something just to curb his appetite. When Measley first started at the school, he was married with two children, and was a trim 215 pounds. By the end of his seventh year he weighed 285 pounds, was divorced, and his health was fading. He was often out sick, and when he was present, he seemed tired and lifeless.

Test scores and student achievement moved in an upward direction during his first five years, but from year six onward, a downward spiral started to occur. At the end of his tenth year, the superintendent decided not to renew Measley's contract mainly due to the reduction of student achievement and his excessive absences.

Essential Questions: Was the law followed in the above scenario? Why or why not? If yes, what actions did the principal take to adhere to the law? If not, what should the principal have done in order to have been more effective? What did you learn from the scenario? Would you do anything differently?

Chapter Two

Law 2: Learn the Culture of the School and Community

This law is a must for all school leaders. It is not only essential to one's survival in the urban school principalship, but is also important for understanding the district, the students, and the community in which the school is located. The information you'll learn from understanding the culture of these three will be invaluable.

Failure to follow this law will make your time in the urban principalship very difficult. You will be in the dark about issues connected with your school, causing you to make bad decisions unnecessarily.

YOUR SURVIVAL

Urban education, and public education as a whole, is a highly emotional and politically charged arena. The higher you climb up the administrative ladder, the more you will be exposed to its real nature. People on the outside are usually unaware of how the field of education can be just as intense, cut-throat, nasty, and hostile as any other high-stakes business environment.

The intense conditions are created from increased emphasis on state standardized testing, depleting school budgets (expecting to do more with less), shrinking student enrollment, low student achievement, increased competition from charter schools, and society's emotional attachment to public education, just to name a few.

Since these conditions are a pervasive part of the urban school landscape, all employees from the superintendent down to the janitorial staff feel pressure (at various levels of course). The pressure is intensified for building-level principals in urban schools because they typically do not have a union, and are not usually offered multiple-year contracts if they're working in a district with a history of failure. Also, the principal's position is arguably the most visible position in the entire school district, behind the superintendent—so scrutiny is at an all-time high.

To make matters worse, administrators in urban districts are transferred or removed from positions without any advance warning or significant reason. This is why understanding the cultural landscape of the district is so important. Your survival as an urban school principal starts with your global knowledge of the school district in which you're working. You must have an expanded view of the issues surrounding the district in relation to your place as a building principal.

This would include, but is not limited to, the following: learning about the district's student academic performance in previous years, history and relationship with the community, student information (i.e., ethnic background, number of English-language learners, number of students qualifying for free and reduced lunches, number of students with disabilities, scores on standardized tests, graduation rates), past and present achievements, the manner in which administrators are treated, salaries in relation to other districts of similar size, stance on student discipline, the history and relationship with the teachers' union, most current levies attempted and passed, stance on engaging parents and the community, well-known or publicized scandals and taboos, suspension and expulsion rates, past successes and failures of previous principals, and the overall climate of the school district. To acquire such information, you have to do a little research, listen to people around you, and ask plenty of questions.

Remember: no two school districts are alike. Whenever you are employed by a school district, there will be a multitude of rules that govern behavior. You must respect the values, judgments, networks, relationships, and patterns of behavior already established before you were hired. You don't have to agree with all of them, but you must respect them if you want to get things done for your school.

In the absence of a keen understanding of your district's cultural norms, you will make mistakes and cause people to alienate you. Before you know it, you'll be in a terrible situation and be totally oblivious as to how you got there. With deep knowledge of your district's cultural norms, you'll be able to navigate through and avoid many of the pitfalls. You'll also be better able to work the system for your school's advantage. Trying to work without such cultural knowledge is literally committing career suicide.

THE SCHOOL AND COMMUNITY

In warfare, a good general or strategist must have a keen understanding of all factors associated with the battle. He/she must have a sound knowledge of the landscape, weather conditions, the number and morale of the enemy's soldiers in comparison to his/her own, and the resources supporting the war, just to name a few. The best military generals try to expand their knowledge and learn all the pieces of the puzzle before waging war. Urban/inner-city school principals should learn a thing or two from military generals because learning the culture of the school and community isn't much different.

Principals should learn as much as possible about the school's culture before stepping foot into the school building. You can't restrict your knowledge to merely knowing who does what in the school. You must learn the history of the school, traditions, celebrations, heroes and heroines, statistics (graduation rates, student attendance, staff attendance, discipline referrals and suspensions), staff morale, types of school programs and how they function, employee retention rates, and more.

Next, you will need to become knowledgeable about the communities from which the students come. According to Wiles and Bondi (1998), when gathering information about the people who live in the area served by the school district, an attempt should be made to understand the educational and cultural levels of the community, general attitudes about the schools, and expectations for education in the area.

The school is nothing more than an extension of the community in which it is located. Most communities that are flourishing have people in them that have good paying jobs, nice housing, ample recreation, sufficient health care, and low crime. As a result of the community's stability, the schools within these communities are successful and flourishing as well. On the opposite end, schools located in neighborhoods with high crime, unemployment, substandard housing and health care, and violence will generally mirror the same issues of that community. Individuals do not automatically change their mentality upon entering the doors of the school. The latter example generally describes urban schools and neighborhoods.

Urban school principals need to understand the factors affecting the communities from which their students come because this will allow them to build connections, establish rapport, develop mechanisms that will reform the school, and stop some of the potential problems. Principals need to learn community information such as crime statistics, types of housing and environmental conditions, employment rates, average household income, demographic information, the community's relationship with the school/district, and recent events and festivals.

When trying to learn the cultural norms of the school and community, you need to totally submerge yourself in it. Study every aspect very closely. For example, if the community is plagued by gang violence, find out who are the toughest gangs in the neighborhood. Learn everything you can about them (patterns, leaders, structure, colors, dealings, oaths, rituals, symbols, alliances and networks, etc.). If the community has a gang problem, chances are your school will have one as well. Knowing such factors will help guide your decision making when encountering students who are gang affiliated.

When trying to gather information, the Internet is a wonderful source. You can research various articles and view other sources of information you find desirable. Make sure you critically filter through what you find on the Internet, however, because some of the things posted do not come from credible sources.

Even though the Internet is a useful tool, the best way to acquire the information you're looking for is to experience it firsthand. Experiencing the community's culture will tie your knowledge and understanding to something visceral and real. You will not have to rely on the perceptions of others, which usually tend to be distorted and at times unreliable. Having a firsthand understanding is the starting point for all things that follow.

Visit the community and see for yourself. Drive by the neighborhoods and observe the conditions of the buildings and overall environment. Get out of the car and walk around. Go inside a few establishments and look around. Try to see the community through the lens of the residents. Start conversations with people and ask questions. Make your own connections, and establish relationships with those from the community who have a sincere interest in the school's welfare.

Another good idea is to organize a community walk with your staff. This will expose your staff to some of the same experiences you had, and help them to gain a better understanding of the community as well. Experiencing the community for yourself will allow you to be more informed about the needs of your students and the school.

EXAMPLE

Sara Betts was the principal of a middle school containing 450 students. She served in this position for three years. The school had a history of failure before Mrs. Betts arrived, but under her leadership, the school was able to make modest gains. She was able to do this in part by securing the halls, improving instruction through teacher professional development, and making cosmetic changes in the school.

One day the instructional superintendent met with Betts and told her about some of the discussions surrounding a possible merger between her school and a neighboring middle school less than five miles away. When the instructional superintendent asked Betts for her thoughts, she strongly opposed it. She opposed it because, even though there is not much distance between the schools, the students who attend them are very different.

Betts learned of the division between the neighborhoods during the first year of her tenure. She learned that the two neighborhoods are rivals, and have been feuding for several years. The hostility between the two communities was so bad that a student from one neighborhood was brutally beaten and murdered outside of a local skating rink where members from both communities were present.

Betts warned that bringing the two together to form one school would incite community fights and riots under the school's roof. She later met with the superintendent's cabinet and shared the same information. This time she brought newspaper articles and information she discovered on the Internet. She also brought a few parents to the meeting that shared her same sentiments. After hearing Betts's testimony, and those of the parents, the district decided not to combine the students into one school.

Essential Questions: Was the law followed in the above scenario? Why or why not? If yes, what actions did the principal take to adhere to the law? If not, what should the principal have done in order to have been more effective? What did you learn from the scenario? Would you do anything differently?

Chapter Three

Law 3: Become a Supreme Pragmatist

By virtue of your position as principal, there are going to be people who will actively work to gain your trust, confidence, compliance, and assurance. They want you to believe in them and their abilities, to the extent that some will even reveal information (sometimes personal) about others whom they believe do not work as hard, or who are not as committed to their jobs as they claim to be.

There are others who often try to do favors for the principal, and a host of other "nice" things. For example, I've known principals who've had employees and others within the school community offer to buy their lunch, shower them with pleasantries and compliments, and/or frequently volunteer to help with special projects within and around the school.

Some of the people who fall in this category may truly believe in you as a school leader, and your vision for reforming the school, while others are trying to get you to let down your guard and lull you into believing they're something they're not. How should urban school principals determine the real from the fake? The sincere from the sinister? The ones who want to support versus the ones who want to sabotage? Principals should make that determination by operating pragmatically.

Don't be swayed by niceness and random acts of kindness from the people around you. Urban school principals can't let smiles and smooth words blind them from what people are really doing (or not doing) in their school buildings. Urban school principals must judge all people and situations based on the results they produce. Look at their deeds, and pay less attention to their words.

People will give you a song and dance in an effort to mask their true intentions, and/or to hide their deficiencies. They will give you a lot of lip service in order to have you think they're doing a good job, but in reality they're not. Don't fall for it! Their words are nothing more than hot air unless they can be backed by results. They deliver this lip homage to you in an effort to gain your trust. Gaining your trust will allow them to continue to operate under the usual status quo. If you take a pragmatic approach to leadership, you will pay less attention to what a person is saying and more attention to a person's actions and the results those actions produce.

In order to reform urban schools into viable institutions of learning, principals need to stress accountability. Principals must spearhead a culture that's evidence based and results oriented. This is the pragmatic way. The best way to do this is to use various forms of data, and share such information with your staff.

When most people hear the word "data," they tend to conjure up images of some high-level scientific experiment or case study. In actuality, data is used in a lot of practical ways. Many school districts across America are starting to use various forms of data to help improve instruction and to evaluate teaching practices. Principals should also determine the types of data they want to collect for their individual schools, and use that data as a foundation for moving forward.

Incorporating the use of data helps schools to create a clear vision for student learning, and to reach maximum student achievement. Using data also helps principals to focus on set goals and targeted areas of improvement, therefore allowing them to evaluate the impact that instructional strategies have on student achievement. The different forms of data collected will help to uncover patterns and relationships in various aspects of school operations, and give principals the most accurate information possible, which will help to inform decision making. Principals can adjust curriculum practices based on the information received in order to meet whatever goals that have been chosen.

No longer should principals continue practices and methods simply because that's how people have always done it. Decisions should be made based on tangible evidence (data). The evidence should determine whether a practice, person, or strategy is useful to the school or not. The use of data can be an effective way to boost student achievement. It forces the school's staff to grapple with their assumptions about teaching and learning within their school, and critically evaluate their own effectiveness at delivering quality instruction. Doing so will plainly show whether or not their assumptions match reality.

People can talk all they want, but the proof is in the pudding. The numbers don't lie. Analyzing data will not only help you to move instruction, but it is also an effective means to determine which programs (or individuals) are the most effective.

Incompetence should be terminated immediately. In regard to ineffective programs, determine what's getting in the way of positive results and try to create a solution. If fixing the problem is not feasible, then terminate the program altogether and start from scratch.

The same holds true for incompetent staff members. After determining the issue affecting a person's performance, try to provide assistance to help him/her get better. Make sure you document everything. If the person shows no signs of improvement after a sufficient amount of time has been given and resources allocated, then that person has to go as well. You should follow the necessary steps to have that person removed from your school building. It's that simple.

Many urban school administrators can't operate pragmatically because they let their friendships, acquaintances, and relationships they've established with individuals get in the way of their sound judgment. They're ruled too heavily by their emotions, so they're not able to separate business from friendship. School principals who fall into this category are a detriment to their school, students, staff, and themselves.

To some, the pragmatic approach might seem too direct and too cruel. Many principals who do not operate in a results-driven fashion tend to place ineffective people in the role of a victim. They make excuses for the inefficiency and neglect, and allow such staff members more opportunities than are necessary to change and improve their practices, or they do nothing and let the incompetent staff person operate with impunity.

I would ask those school leaders who allow such nonsense to take place in their schools: What about the students who are affected by a staff person's ineffectiveness? Why should the students suffer because a staff member or program couldn't produce the desired outcomes after receiving adequate assistance and/or support? Think of how the ineffectiveness will affect the overall functioning of the school.

Principals are the caretakers of the educational experiences of every student who attends school. Think of the irreversible damage ineffective people cause students year after year in urban/inner-city schools. Too often, more attention is placed on saving the job of ineffective employees than is placed on thinking about the needs of the suffering students. This is one of the reasons why urban schools are in such bad condition. If the work of school-level employees doesn't benefit students, then those employees shouldn't be associated with the school.

Being a supreme pragmatist means looking at people and programs within the school honestly. It means measuring situations and individual actions as they are, and not as what you would like them to be. Urban school principals must get in the habit of judging people by results, and not according to friendliness or political capital. Working in this manner will allow you to move the school forward and out of the trappings of failure and mediocrity.

EXAMPLE

Mr. Stevenson is a first-year principal at a high school of 800 students, grades 9 through 12. He had been a principal for six years at the middle school level prior to making the jump to high school. The high school received a poor rating on its state report card in previous years.

Stevenson was hired in order to move the school from its failing status. Immediately after accepting the position, Stevenson began to collect data on the school's programs and test scores. He noticed that math scores were significantly lower than the English scores.

Based on the data, he realized that improvements in math, along with moderate success in English, would lift the school from a rating of ineffective to one of continuous improvement. While surveying the school's programs, he discovered that the school has a partnership with a local nonprofit organization. The nonprofit company had been responsible for after-school tutoring in math over the past three years. It received a three-year grant with an annual award of $50,000 for providing tutoring services for the high school.

The organization's liaison with the school is Mr. Green. Stevenson met with Green to discuss his organization's involvement with the school. At the meeting, Green displayed his own data, which indicated that over 300 different students received tutoring after school, and 95 percent of those students scored "advanced" on their in-house assessments. Stevenson was very skeptical of Green's data, so he decided to investigate. He asked several math teachers about Green's involvement with the school and the tutors his organization used.

It turns out that none of the math teachers in the department have ever seen any outside tutors in the building. He also discovered that Green rarely came into the building himself, and when he did come, he spent most of his time in Mrs. Jacob's classroom. Jacob and Green attend the same church. Jacob was the one who linked Green's organization with the former principal.

Stevenson scheduled another meeting with Green and told him that the organization's services were no longer needed. The principal had elected to use the school's math teachers to do the after-school tutoring instead. Green argued with Stevenson, informing him that if his organization left the school, it would no longer be eligible for the grant it was receiving.

Green went on to share how the money received from the grant was a vital source of funding for his organization. Stevenson remained steadfast, outlining the discrepancies in his data. He also let Green know that based on the math scores from the state's report card, the tutoring hadn't been effective and was not benefiting the needs of the school.

Green became upset and threatened to contact the superintendent. Stevenson did not change his mind. Green left the principal's office very disgruntled. That was the last conversation between the two men and the nonprofit organization did not resume their services to the school.

Essential Questions: Was the law followed in the above scenario? Why or why not? If yes, what actions did the principal take to adhere to the law? If not, what should the principal have done in order to have been more effective? What did you learn from the scenario? Would you do anything differently?

Chapter Four

Law 4: Establish Your Authority

Some school leaders would argue that today's principals have very little power and authority compared to what principals had in previous years. Many believe that most of the principal's authority has been stripped away over time by various groups such as teachers' unions, Parent-Teacher Associations (PTAs), Local School Decision Making Committees (LSDMCs), state and federal mandates, and various central office personnel.

Despite the many opposing forces threatening the principal's authority, urban school principals can still establish and maintain authority within the school setting. In fact, it's imperative that they do so if they want to get anything accomplished, and survive in the position.

New principals need to establish their authority because they are entering a building where there are preexisting alliances, relationships, and ties. The staff may already look toward others who've been in the school building previously as authority figures, especially those who may have a prolonged history with the school. That may not necessarily be a bad thing for a new principal, unless the staff member who holds the employees' affections is not willing to adjust to any changes or initiatives from the principal.

Experienced principals could also have an authority problem, and may need to reaffirm themselves. There are signs that will tell experienced principals if they lack proper authority. Experienced principals should ask themselves the following questions to see if they have an authority problem: Are people frequently absent from meetings initiated by the principal without a legitimate excuse, or are they chronically late? When in meetings, are people having sidebar conversations, grading papers, or texting while the principal is talking? When in the halls, do students walk past the principal having inappropriate conversations because they either are unaware, or don't care, that the principal is in their presence? When asked to provide important documents or to complete a designated task, do staff members move slothfully and without any sense of urgency? Do subordinates openly defy the principal in front of others? Are the principal's initiatives ignored by those who should be carrying out tasks? If the answer is yes to more than one of the above questions, then the principal has an authority issue.

Establishing your authority is important because you are the person whom the district has placed in charge of the school. You can defer, delegate, and ask for input from others, but the bottom line is that you are responsible. Anything that happens within the school is under your watch. Other individuals in the building who act like they have supreme authority by virtue of their time employed with the school (or district) will not be the ones called to task by the superintendent when test scores don't improve, or about any other important matter.

Urban schools are crippled by people working within them who do not perform their job duties adequately or have an inflated view of their importance, position, and/or status. In some urban schools, there are too many chiefs and not enough indians. As principal, you are the chief, so claim your rightful position.

Urban school principals can establish (or reestablish) their authority, first by taking the principalship seriously, and second by increasing their visibility within the school. Doing so will help you gain the authoritative power needed to get people moving, and to get things done.

BE SERIOUS

You must let everyone know how serious you are about education, and about your role as the school's principal. Your passion, enthusiasm, and seriousness should be easily detected in your actions and words. At your very first staff meeting, and every chance thereafter, you must espouse your beliefs and strongest convictions about teaching and learning. You must also share with your staff your honest assessment of the school and how you're willing to do whatever is necessary to get things moving in the right direction.

After sharing your beliefs and your passion for the position, you're going to have to follow those words with stern actions. Words combined with action are a powerful combination. Your staff, and nearly everyone you come in contact with, is going to scrutinize everything you say and do. The words you say out of your mouth must be aligned with your actions.

For example, if you say you're going to tackle student discipline, then that's what people should see. If you say you're going to put an end to students cutting classes and walking the halls, then the staff will be observing to see if you're going to follow through. If you speak out against employee tardiness, then don't be tardy to meetings or to work yourself.

The same holds true for your statements regarding improving student achievement, decreasing suspensions, improving graduation rates, and so on. Your words should be seen in every aspect of your actions, from budget allocations to hiring personnel—and everything in between.

INCREASE YOUR VISIBILITY

The urban school principalship is not a position in which you can play from afar. There are no ivory towers from which to look down. You can't lock yourself in the office or hide out in some remote part of the building and still be effective. You have to be visible, up close, and personal with the people and surroundings that impact your school.

Many urban school principals make the mistake of spending too much time in their offices talking on the phone, answering emails, or meeting with people who can't advance the school's mission. Staying in the office will make some people down in central happy, but it will not turn the school into a productive place for students and teachers.

Being seen is the best way to establish and maintain authority in the eyes of everyone (students, teachers, parents, and visitors). Increased visibility is good for the principal because he/she is able to stay abreast of what's going on within the school from one second to the next. It will also help the principal develop a firsthand understanding of what people are doing or not doing.

Principals should be seen in the halls when students are passing between classes, inside classrooms while instruction is taking place, during students' arrival and dismissal times, during lunch periods, sporting events, PTA meetings (when appropriate), assemblies, in the basement, locker rooms, parking lot, and so on. Any place in the school building where people frequently visit is a place the principal should become familiar with.

While you're out and about, give out correction or praise to a student or staff member. This action will also add to your authority in the eyes of those watching. Your constant presence will keep people on their toes. It will also give some a sense of confidence. The confidence will come from knowing that the principal (head authority figure) is somewhere in the vicinity in case there is trouble.

The bottom line is that the principal is the one ultimately responsible for anything that does, or does not, happen in the school. You want to establish your authority, not so people can become afraid of you, or to become a dictator, but in order to get things done in the proper manner. You want to let people know how much you hate stagnation, complacency, ineffectiveness, and mediocrity.

The principal must let everyone know that such adverse characteristics will no longer be tolerated under his/her watch. Doing so gives the people under their direction clear expectations, and will let them know the standards for job performance.

Most school buildings will generally take on the characteristics of the leader. If the leader has a carefree, hands-off approach to governing the school, then the people working under the leader will mirror the same attitude. In contrast, if the principal shows how serious and passionate he/she is with words and actions to match, then the staff will rally and follow suit.

Your actions will also work toward erasing any confusion about who has the most power and authority in the building. Without authority, the principal is no different from any other person in the school building. A principal with authority translates into a principal with respect. If your school's staff respects you, then they will work hard for you. If you are not respected, then the end result is chaos.

Understand—if you're the principal in an urban school district, it is inevitable that you are going to bump heads with someone who thinks they have more authority than you do. The person may come in the form of an assistant principal, dean, teacher, PTA president, counselor, or one of the support staff. In their particular spheres, they have been given a bit of clout and power by their peers.

They may have become so drunk with adoration, arrogance, pride, and haughtiness that they feel confident enough to step out of their position and challenge the principal in a negative manner. Their inflated view of their own importance also stems from previous principals' failure to effectively deal with them when they first began to show this side of their character.

Do not avoid these people. Avoiding the conflict will signal to them, and the rest of the staff, that the individual(s) opposing you really does have power and authority. It will make you look weak and confirm the distorted notions that exist about the opposition's perceived power, importance, and authority. Do not hesitate. Challenge them head on, no matter who it is. You have to put an end to their mischief before their behavior spreads throughout the staff like cancer.

When someone negatively challenges the principal's authority, the principal must deal with them in a strategic manner. Don't get emotional or engage in a shouting match in public. Doing so will only bring you down to their level. The best way to convince people is not through argument, but by actions.

The first step is to give out reprimands. Write them up for insubordination (or whatever area of negligence their actions fall under). Reprimands are linked to most employees' evaluation and job performance. Too many could result in demotion, salary decreases, suspension, and/or termination.

After the reprimands have been issued, the next step would be to remove their power source. You must separate them from the thing or the people that gives them the illusion of authority. This is done by cutting off their resources, hacking away at their supports, reducing their responsibilities that are outside of their normal job descriptions, decreasing their visibility within the school, or restricting their access to places in the building.

Do whatever is legally necessary so that they understand their true place and authority in relation to yours. You want to administer a persistent attack that will make them fold under the pressure, and acknowledge their fallibility. The goal is to make them so uncomfortable that they can't bear to continue working in the climate you've created for them. They will have to surrender to your authority, or find a new school to work in.

I know what I've just stated will not be found in most school leadership books. Some may judge the above strategies as a misuse of power, but it really isn't. Divided leadership is one of the easiest ways of preventing a school from moving forward. If urban school principals do not confront those that oppose their authority and leadership, the cancer will spread throughout the school—infecting everyone.

Trying to talk opponents into following your lead and respecting your position will not work, because your reforms for improvement threaten their very existence. They want to continue operating in the old climate because it was the old climate that led to them attaining their power. A softer, prolonged approach will hurt the school's leadership because no one will listen to, or follow, the principal's lead—making him/her ineffective. People do not respect weak leadership. Dealing with those that challenge your authority in a strategic manner will also reinforce your authority with the rest of the staff.

There will always be those on your staff who despise the rabble-rousers, but they're part of the silent minority. They are waiting for someone with the courage to stand up and declare what's right. Seeing your tough stance with someone perceived to be a respected figure will cement your credibility and weaken your opponent's. It will also prevent any future challenges from others.

Final note: principals should also understand that just because someone asks questions, or offers contrasting opinions, doesn't mean that they're trying to challenge the principal's authority. Sometimes the principal will face challenges simply because the initiative, directions, tasks, or policies do not make sense to some staff members/stakeholders, or expectations might be unclear. The sincere types are not trying to be defiant or disrespectful. They want transparency, and openness, that will allow them to fulfill their duties effectively and serve the school in the best possible manner. The challenges and questions that come from them are healthy because these lead to positive dialogue and growth, and provide clarity.

EXAMPLE

Tammy Wheeling became principal of an elementary school after serving four years as the school's assistant principal. Patricia Steel was a veteran teacher at the school. Steel worked in the school for 20 years.

Steel gained a lot of respect from other teachers because she was very outspoken, and had a reputation for being tough when it came to student discipline and classroom management. She was also chairperson of the Best Practices Committee, which was a very influential position in the school (the chairperson is paid an additional sum of $1,500 per year). During the course of her tenure at the school, Steel worked under seven different principals— Mrs. Wheeling was going to make the eighth.

When Wheeling was an assistant principal, she noticed how Steel seemed to undermine reform initiatives from the former principal by making spectacles in staff meetings, disrespectfully challenging the principal openly, and using the teachers' union contract as her excuse for what she will and will not do. Steel was never satisfied with anything. Nothing was good enough. Every idea for change was a bad one as far as she was concerned, but she would complain vehemently about the leadership's inability to improve low test scores and about overall school inefficiencies.

One of the first things Wheeling did as principal was to initiate a meeting with Steel. The purpose was to let Steel know that she wanted to promote open lines of communication, and to get Steel's input as to how they could collaboratively make the school better. The meeting lasted only five or six minutes. Steel told Wheeling to do whatever she felt was necessary, just don't get in her way or bother her.

When the school year started, Wheeling assigned lunch/recess duties for teachers on a rotational basis. Everything was fine during the first three weeks. During weeks four and five, Wheeling noticed that some teachers were not reporting to their lunch/recess duties. When confronted, each teacher stated that they didn't have to do it. They all said Mrs. Steel told them that lunch/recess duty was a violation of their contract so they didn't have to do that if they didn't want to.

Steel was not abreast of the changes made to the teachers' contract during the collective bargaining that took place at the end of last school year. One of the changes gave principals the authority to assign non-teaching tasks such as lunch duty to teachers, as long as it didn't exceed a certain number per month.

Wheeling received a copy of the teachers' new contract and highlighted the portion that pertained to lunch/recess duties. She also gave each teacher a verbal warning for not following the school's policy. She also let them know that any future occurrences would be considered willful neglect of duty, which could lead to reprimands, suspensions, and possible termination of employment if the issue continued. The teachers got the message and followed the schedule accordingly.

Next, Wheeling went to Steel with a highlighted copy of the teachers' contract. Steel read it but refused to follow it—stating that she wasn't going to do it regardless of what the contract said. When it was Steel's turn to do recess duty, she did not report. She didn't show up for recess duty for an entire month. Each time she missed her scheduled days, Wheeling wrote her up for willful neglect of duty. Wheeling also removed Steel from her position as chairperson of the Best Practices Committee, and replaced her with Mr. O'Conner. O'Conner was also a veteran teacher, but he was more collegial and willing to do whatever was necessary for the students and the school. According to the newly revised teachers' contract, it was up to the principal's discretion to appoint a new chairperson of a committee if the current chairperson receives two or more written reprimands in one fiscal year.

Since Steel had more than two written reprimands, Wheeling decided to replace her. The decision to remove Steel as chairperson enraged her, causing her to file a grievance against Wheeling. The entire school knew about the situation. Many staff members stayed clear of Steel because they didn't want to become associated with such a controversial situation. Most of the staff members only wanted to do their jobs and serve the needs of the students.

Steel's grievance was heard and then thrown out. The hearing officer stated that the claim against Principal Wheeling was unfounded and lacked sufficient evidence to be credible. Steel was also made to do lunch/recess duty like the other teachers. While the grievance issues were taking place, the school's staff (other than Steel) began to work collaboratively and more cohesively.

Without the adoration and following of certain staff members, Steel became a non-issue. She stopped speaking out, being disrespectful, and challenging every idea for positive change. Since she didn't have the chairperson position to use as a personal platform, Steel was unable to affect the staff as before. At the end of the school year, Steel requested to be transferred to another school. The request was granted.

Essential Questions: Was the law followed in the above scenario? Why or why not? If yes, what actions did the principal take to adhere to the law? If not, what should the principal have done in order to have been more effective? What did you learn from the scenario? Would you do anything differently?

Chapter Five

Law 5: At Times, Be Unpredictable

After you have worked to establish yourself, your staff and students will start to become familiar with you. Familiarity is a good thing, and is certainly something the principal should seek to accomplish, but pretty soon others will start trying to predict your moves, routines, patterns of behavior, and actions. The staff and students will also begin to develop habits, some good and others bad, based on their perception of your activity (or inactivity).

Some of your staff will put on a dog-and-pony show when you're around, but when you're gone they will go back to old habits and ineffective practices. This kind of behavior is often typical of people who are not fully acclimated to new systems or fully adjusted to the changes going on around them. As the saying goes, "When the cat is away, the mice will play."

Being predictable gives some staff members, like the ones mentioned above, a sense of control and comfort. This type of comfort is not only restricted to ineffective staff members, it can also be seen from students as well. For example, if students notice a pattern of hall sweeps being conducted only during periods three and five, then they will hurry to classes during those times to avoid a consequence, but they will linger in the halls or take their time getting to classes during other periods. Students will also try to cut classes, and attempt all sorts of mischievous behaviors in various parts of the school building, if they believe the administrative presence is weak in certain areas.

The urban school principal must turn the tide—be deliberately unpredictable. Varying your patterns, routines, and behaviors after you've established yourself will keep people off balance and guessing what you will do next. People will not be able to calculate your moves or foresee your actions. Their preconceived notions about you will shatter when you do something out of the ordinary that they weren't expecting.

Principals should play a constant game of inserting themselves and then deliberately withdrawing. When people expect to see you, they will not. But when they don't expect you, that's when you should appear. This will give you the advantage and increase your authority as well.

Your capriciousness will give you a true sense of what people are doing when you're not around. If you pop up at odd moments and see a staff member working diligently, then chances are that person works diligently all the time. But if you see a staff person working hard when you're around, but slacking when you appear unannounced, then that person is the one who probably slacks all the time.

Each time you notice a slacker, you should have a conversation with that person about their behavior and work ethic. If the problems persist, then the principal should strategically attack the problem or the undesirable behavior. In doing so, you will either help the person(s) to get better, or help them out the door. Either way, they're going to get help.

EXAMPLE

Michael Stun has been a high school principal for seven years. He was able to lead his school out of a continuous improvement rating, to a proficient one. One of the tactics he used to move his school forward was to visit at least five classrooms per day, for a minimum of five minutes.

Every day of the school year, Mr. Stun would go into classrooms to observe instruction. No one knew which classrooms he would visit, but all the teachers who had been with the school since he arrived knew that he would be popping up somewhere. One day Stun walked into Mrs. White's ninth grade English class during second period. White was a first-year teacher. When Stun walked in, the class had been in session for 20 minutes. White was sitting behind her desk while the students were having casual conversations with each other, with no visible assignment in front of them.

Stun sat down in an empty chair located in back of the room. When White noticed the principal entering the room, she immediately jumped up and walked to the front of the class, and asked the class to turn their books to page 33. Stun noticed that many of the students didn't have their books. Also, many of them seemed to be surprised by White's sudden interest in delivering a lesson. After about 10 or 15 minutes of watching White try to bluff her way through a lesson, Stun left the room.

Stun returned to White's classroom to observe her third period class. This time when he walked in, White was at her desk again, but this time on her computer. Again, when she saw the principal come into the room, she left the computer and tried to bluff her way through another lesson. This time, one of the students shouted, "Mrs. White, you know we weren't doing nothing before the principal came in. Why you tryin' to act like we was?" White ignored the student's comment and continued with what she was doing.

The next day, Stun had a meeting with White to discuss his observations. He also outlined the school's expectations and confirmed her understanding. Over the course of the school year, White's students consistently scored lower on common assessments than students of other teachers in the same subject area.

She also displayed poor planning and insufficient teaching practices, despite being assigned a teacher mentor and given multiple attempts for professional development. According to the district's teaching contract, all first-year teachers are under probation. This means that if the principal can demonstrate through evidence that the person is inadequate, the school district doesn't have to renew his/her contract. At the end of the school year, Stun made the recommendation for nonrenewal, so White was released from the district.

Essential Questions: Was the law followed in the above scenario? Why or why not? If yes, what actions did the principal take to adhere to the law? If not, what should the principal have done in order to have been more effective? What did you learn from the scenario? Would you do anything differently?

Chapter Six

Law 6: Create a Loyal Cabinet

Law 6 is a very import law for urban school principals. A principal's cabinet is made up of individuals who have a great deal invested in the school, and want to see it succeed. These people give suggestions, offer opinions, provide insight, and/or advise the principal on policies and issues that affect the school. Principals should hold regular meetings with the cabinet in order to discuss important school issues, dispense information, or to receive feedback.

Urban school principals have to make a lot of high-level, important decisions about the school, and/or its stakeholders, on a daily basis. They need people around them who are loyal, committed, and able to aid the principal in making some of the tough decisions. A principal's cabinet should be made up of supporters from inside and outside of the school.

Members of the cabinet should come from a combination of the following areas: assistant principals, teachers or other school leaders, and members of the surrounding community. What follows is a description of each group, and how they can effectively serve as part of the principal's cabinet.

ASSISTANT PRINCIPALS

Of all the staff members working in a school, assistant principals are the closest to the principal. They are a part of the school's administrative team, and they work directly under the principal's leadership. Hiring the right assistant principal(s) could be compared to a person marrying the right spouse. Choose wisely and your days will be lived happily ever after, but if you choose incorrectly, it will be a living hell all the days you are married.

Good assistant principals are good not only for the school's success, but also for the principal's individual success as well. The assistant principals are the lieutenants who carry out the general's (principal's) plans and overall reform, policies, procedures, and initiatives. They also serve as additional eyes and ears throughout the school.

Principals are not able to manage, supervise, or oversee everything that goes on within the school building at all times. Your assistants are able to be in places and see things when you are not able to. They will also serve as your pipeline for information because they will often be more accessible than you are. Principals must hire, and/or develop, the best individuals possible to fill the assistant principal role.

When choosing your assistant principals, you want to select those that share your ideas of school reform, and your values about education. You also want them to be positive, self-motivated individuals who can think on their own. The idea is to select people who have character, backbone, and intelligence. You don't want to hire clones or robots to obey your every command. That will not benefit you or the school.

It is a good practice for principals to hire assistants who have strengths in areas where they have weakness. For example, if student discipline is not the principal's specialty, then he/she should hire an assistant who is more of a disciplinarian. If the principal isn't good with using technology, then an assistant principal who is technologically savvy would be very beneficial.

Think about your strengths and weaknesses as a principal, and what the school needs overall. The assistant principal(s) should be able to fill the administrative void(s). In doing so, principals will select assistants who complement their leadership, making the principal and the entire school more effective.

If you are a new principal to a school, and you've inherited assistant principals who have been in the school building longer, then you must immediately find out where they stand. It is normal to assume they'll have some affection toward the former principal, especially if the former principal was well liked. It is also safe to assume that an assistant principal could have applied for the head position, but wasn't selected. He/she could be harboring some resentment because of it.

Another possibility is that the former principal didn't use his assistant principal(s) effectively. In cases such as this, assistants spent a good portion of their time on areas of little importance, or they may have developed bad habits that contributed to the dysfunction of the school. This means that the new principal will have to retrain the assistants, and get them working in a manner that is productive. It is vital that the school's administrative team be in accord at the start and end of the school year.

If your assistants have been in the building before you, then you have to quickly get them on board with your leadership vision by sharing your convictions and attitudes about education, and your ideas for change within the school—while also expressing how they fit into the overall scheme. Solicit their thoughts and opinions and listen to what they have to say. Dialogue with them about what should be improved within the school. If your assistants have been in the building longer than you, they should have acquired valuable knowledge about relationships and patterns of behavior in and around the school. This information will be invaluable to you as principal.

Next, whether the assistants are new or not, assign each one specific tasks, duties, and responsibilities. Clearly outline the expectations for their performance, and confirm their understanding. After specific duties have been given, monitor them to see how they perform their tasks.

Observe their work ethic and ask yourself the following questions: Do they meet deadlines? Are they timely? Do they work well with others? Do they show initiative? Can they stand up under pressure? Do they carry a positive attitude and disposition? Do students and staff respect them? Are they able to multitask? Are they able to get things done? Do they show good leadership skills? Do they keep their word? Are they quick learners? Do they frequently offer good opinions and ideas? Are they dependable? Could I (the principal) feel comfortable leaving the building knowing my assistant(s) are in charge in my absence?

If your assistants (whether experienced or not) perpetuate too many of the negative characteristics that you are fighting to change within the school building, then you have to either correct the adverse characteristics, or work to remove them as soon as possible. Assistant principals are a direct reflection of the principal's leadership. If they are ineffective, then you will look ineffective. Failure to correct, or remove, an assistant principal will have negative consequences on the school's overall success.

It is a lot easier to remove an ineffective assistant principal than it is to remove an inadequate teacher, because administrators typically don't have strong unions to protect them. This may sound harsh, but it's your job as principal to have a successful school, not to support people who will get in the way of that success. If you don't remove inadequate assistant principals as soon as possible, they will cause mass confusion, divide your leadership, diminish the authority of the school's administration, contribute to the overall ineffectiveness of the school, and assist those who are set on keeping the status quo of failure/low performance.

Don't make the mistake of many principals by selecting assistants solely based on their resume, years of experience, or by the degree they hold. You want to make your decision based upon the person's overall character, their philosophy about education, and their views about working with the urban student population. A person of strong character will be better able to overcome adversity when faced with it. They will not fold when the tough issues and situations of working in an urban school arise. Choosing the right assistants will make the principal look good overall, but choosing the wrong ones could put the entire administration, and the success of the school, in jeopardy.

TEACHERS/OTHER SCHOOL LEADERS

The principal's cabinet should also be made up of teachers and other school leaders. Other school leaders could come from members of the school's support staff (counselors, office workers, custodians, aides, psychologist, program coordinators, resource specialists, etc.). Some leaders will become evident by their work habits, skills, and job acumen. Other leaders will stand out once they've been given the chance to show what they can do. Either way, the principal must recognize who these individuals are, and tap into their knowledge in order to help transform the school.

Leaders who come from these groups are important for two main reasons: first, they serve as role models for those who are in their peer group. For example, a teacher who is punctual, responsible, dedicated, and diligent in all of his/her duties will transfer those same qualities to others around them. Also, if this same teacher has some clout or influence, then his/her colleagues will follow the standard that individual has set.

The principal wouldn't have to do a lot of monitoring and checking to make sure the employees are on task because the leaders in that particular group will set the standard and serve as the model of excellence. Furthermore, these types of school leaders will be in places and hear about things that the principal would never be privy to. The information they share could be invaluable.

Second, members from these groups should be part of the principal's cabinet because they have a stake in what goes on in the school, and have a vested interest in the school's success. Therefore, the principal should give members of these groups a voice in the decision-making process, and allow them to contribute to the things that matter to them. Many principals are uncomfortable with giving members of their school community a say in the decision-making process because they fear it will give up too much of their control. In actuality, the exact opposite is true.

Giving stakeholders a chance to voice their opinions about how things should go within the school shows how strong of a school leader you are. You don't lose authority or control by doing this; you actually gain more authority and control because the stakeholders who are taking part in the decision-making process are becoming even more tied to the school. Therefore they become viscerally connected, which will cause them to work even harder to see the school become successful. They will also become more loyal and connected to you for giving them the opportunity to share their thoughts and opinions.

The stakeholders among teachers and other school leaders will inform the principal's decision making, and help him/her acquire an accurate pulse of the overall school culture and climate.

COMMUNITY MEMBERS

No one has a more vested interest in the success of a school than members of the community where the school is located. As mentioned previously, the school is nothing more than an extension of the community, so it is only right that the principal should have a community member(s) on his/her decision-making team. A community member could be a parent, business owner, community organizer, or anyone who wants to work for the benefit of the neighborhood.

Just like with the teacher leaders, community members are privy to information about the community and its residents that almost never reaches the school principal's ears—information that could impact the school and its staff members. Having someone from the community on your cabinet/leadership team will increase the likelihood that such information will be revealed—information that could inform the principal's decision making, and lead to better school operations.

Community members are also helpful when the principal wants to convey information to the community. Community cabinet members are connected, so they are able to dispense information in the right way to those who need to hear it. They are also able to translate the school's messages so that a wide variety of people will be able to understand. This will also strengthen the principal's ties and community networks, and close the distance that often exists between the school and the urban community it serves.

Final note: with any school staff, there will be certain people that will rise above the pack. Their work ethic, persistence, personality, knowledge, and/or leadership qualities will set them apart from the rest. These individuals may come in many forms (teachers, aides, office staff, clerks, parents, community stakeholders, students, etc.).

It will serve the principal well to stay in close contact with these individuals. They will hear conversation and be in places that you, and your assistants, will not be able to reach no matter how connected you might be. They will be able to supply you with invaluable information that can help shape your decision making.

EXAMPLE

Mrs. Baker is a veteran principal of a large elementary school. Entering her twelfth year, she hired two new assistant principals. One was a first-year assistant, while the other had three years of experience in the position at another school district.

Most of her staff members and principal colleagues were shocked that she elected to hire assistants with so little experience, especially since there were two veteran assistants who had been in the district for 12 and 15 years respectively. Baker always took pride in being a good judge of character and talent. She also understood the needs of her school, and knew the types of administrators she needed in order to move forward.

Baker knew the veteran assistants were too nice, too soft, and too chummy with various members of the teaching staff—which she felt would hinder progress in the school building. She figured they would allow their personal relationships with individuals to affect their judgment and soften their stance on the tough issues. This is why she elected to go with the new faces. The new administrators would not have the personal ties that the others had, and they would be willing to work hard since they were still relatively new to the administrative ranks. They still have something to prove.

She met with her new assistant principals individually to find out their strengths and weaknesses. She also assigned them a variety of duties that would give them a broad scope of administrative tasks to build on their current knowledge. Both assistant principals were very competent, enthusiastic, and didn't shy away from a challenge.

There were various times throughout the school year when each assistant principal would take on various tasks that benefited the school greatly. There were also moments when certain individuals on the staff tried to challenge their authority, or bypass the assistant principals and deal directly with the principal. But in every instance, Baker would find out whether the person first communicated with the assistant who took over that particular area of concern.

If the person didn't consult with an assistant principal, Baker would direct them to the one in charge of that issue. This validated the assistants and increased their confidence as well. Baker took a mentoring approach with her assistant principals, and gave them the autonomy to do their jobs as they saw fit just as long as they kept her abreast of their actions beforehand so that she could provide assistance if needed. The assistant principals appreciated Baker's faith and trust in them. This made them work even harder for the school and their principal.

Essential Questions: Was the law followed in the above scenario? Why or why not? If yes, what actions did the principal take to adhere to the law? If not, what should the principal have done in order to have been more effective? What did you learn from the scenario? Would you do anything differently?

II

Moving Forward

Chapter Seven

Law 7: Rally the Troops (Unify the Staff)

There is power in unity. When an institution is unified, the people within it will be bound together by a common cause. Their unity is based upon their shared interest, purpose, beliefs, and values. The tighter the bond between the people of the institution, the more likely the institution will be able to adapt to changes and circumstances as they occur. When institutions are not unified, they can be easily divided, conquered, and/or eliminated by the competition.

Many urban schools do not function in a unified manner, which leads to their overall dysfunction. For example, in some schools the math teachers do not speak to the English teachers. The English teachers do not associate with the science teachers. The science teachers do not like the custodians. The custodians don't care for the office staff, and so on.

Most staff members working in troubled urban schools are disjointed for a couple of reasons. First, the school's leadership hasn't established proper structures for staff communication and collaboration. People are literally doing their "own thing," and there isn't any commonality or consistency within the various school programs or procedures.

Second, due to the school's history of insufficient practices, many staff members have begun to act out of their own self-interest, and not in the best interests of the school as a whole. They have reduced their focus to only what happens on their floor, in their department, or inside their individual classrooms. They've started to function as if they're isolated on an island by themselves without any connections to the people and events around them.

The disconnectedness that many school personnel feel has an adverse affect on other areas of school operations (student discipline, school culture and climate, achievement, collegiality, morale, etc.). Visitors will also be able to sense the disjointed nature of the school because minor issues that could easily be fixed will take an act of Congress to correct. One group of employees will not know what another group is doing due to each group's independent operations.

It is the principal's job as the school's leader to bind the staff together and foster oneness, and create synergy among all the school's employees and its connected parts. The school's staff should be able to understand their connections with each other and with the overall health of the school. Principals must create staff cohesiveness so that all of the school's complex parts work toward the same goals. This is what rallying the troops is all about.

MAKING CONNECTIONS

In order to follow Law 7, urban school principals must effectively communicate to the staff how their individual roles, departments, and responsibilities are connected to the overall success of the school. No matter how insignificant the employees perceive their individual roles to be within the school, they need to be shown the value and importance of their duties in relation to the school's overall success.

For example, when people think of important school personnel, they readily think of teachers or administrative staff. But some of the most valuable school staff members are the custodians. People will form opinions about a school based on its curb appeal and its cleanliness when they walk through the doors. What kind of impression would a visitor have of a school that's dirty and poorly maintained? If a school is not kept properly, parents will not want to send their children there (nor will the students want to come).

If parents explore other options for their children (e.g., home schooling, vouchers, private or religious schools), then student enrollment will go down. If student enrollment diminishes, then there will be cutbacks and layoffs, which translates to loss of jobs for teachers and other employees. This is just one example that demonstrates how all school employees are connected, whether they realize it or not. The same can be said for nearly all positions within a school's professional environment, including office staff and other support personnel. Principals must communicate (early and often) how the school's separate parts connect to move one machine—the school—forward.

METHODS FOR ESTABLISHING UNITY

There are several directions principals can take in order to unify the school's staff. I will discuss four that I find to be the most powerful. First, there is the creation of a mission and/or vision statement. Such statements identify to the world what the school is about and the direction the school is headed.

According to Angelica, a mission statement is a short statement of purpose for a company or organization. Vision statements also define an organization's purpose, but do so in terms of future goals (Angelica, 2001). Both mission and vision statements summarize ideas, goals, and beliefs that the school's staff holds as important and valuable. These statements can be used by school principals to foster unity, shared values, and a common purpose among the staff.

A second method principals can use is the "us versus them" approach. This method involves using the threat of an adversary, opponent, or enemy to bind the staff together. This tactic will force personnel to come together out of survival and necessity. In order for this approach to work, the principal must implement the three key components.

The first component is to identify an enemy. If you don't have an enemy, then you have to create one. Your enemy could be any perceived problem, challenge, person, or issue (e.g., low test scores, central office personnel, student discipline, staff morale, the school board members). It doesn't matter what, or who, the enemy is, just as long as you have something to fight and your staff can somehow visualize whom they're fighting against.

The next component in this approach is to use imagery and creative words to describe your enemy. Give the enemy characteristics that your staff will abhor. This will incite an emotional response that will move them out of their comfort zone and create a sense of urgency. Once out of their comfort zone, they will cling to the leadership (and each other) for safety and security—making the group's needs and desires more important than those of the individuals.

For example, principals should say things like, "They're trying to take us under . . . it seems like they're working against us and our students . . . our survival depends on it . . . either we improve test scores or they're going to reconstitute the school, and who knows where we'll all end up . . . it's now or never, or they'll shut us down . . . we have to protect our children (the students), it's up to us."

Remember: it's okay to exaggerate a little bit, but don't lie. If you're not in danger of being shut down or reconstituted, then don't say it. Make your enemy applicable to your school's current situation. The goal is to merely create some sense of urgency by making your staff a little uncomfortable, which will cause them to unify out of necessity/survival, or to achieve the desired goal.

The final component of this approach is to provide the staff with consistent opportunities to collaborate, dialogue, and strategize to determine the best course of action to defeat the enemy. This will not only help to create a plan to attack the problem at hand, but it will also build solidarity and break down the barriers that once separated them. They will rally around a common purpose to defeat the "enemy."

The only drawback to this approach is that after the staff has accomplished its goal, they will have the tendency to revert back to their previous ways—making the unity experienced short lived. Since the connectedness established will not last very long, principals will constantly have to create new enemies and/or challenges for the staff to overcome. I recommend that you shouldn't overuse this strategy because you never want to keep your staff in a constant state of anxiety. At times, you want them to feel a sense of accomplishment and comfort. This approach is most effective when used sparingly.

A third, longer-lasting approach to unifying a disjointed staff is to create professional learning communities within the school. According to Buffum and Hinman (2006), professional learning communities (PLCs) are extended learning opportunities for teachers and staff that foster collaboration within the school environment. Participants are usually organized in work groups and given opportunities to dialogue, collaborate, construct curriculum, and grapple with important issues that matter to them.

This is very significant because, too often, educators complain about feeling helpless and insignificant, like pawns in a chess game. PLCs put many of the school's decisions in the laps of the group, therefore making them feel empowered and part of a community. When employees feel like they are part of a community, they will be more willing to put the needs of the community first, instead of their own self-interest.

Last, one of the most significant methods for bringing a school's staff together is through interdisciplinary teaming. An interdisciplinary team consists of two or more teachers from different subject areas and the group of students they commonly instruct (Erb and Stevenson, 1999). Team teachers plan, coordinate, and evaluate curriculum and instruction across academic areas. Interdisciplinary teams also cultivate meaningful and regular communication. They often share the same schedule and the same area of the school building. For teachers, teams provide a collaborative and supportive work group.

Interdisciplinary teaming is a useful school organizational structure because it is centered on teachers collaborating, planning, and organizing on behalf of students. Just like PLCs, interdisciplinary teaming is valuable for teachers because it fosters accountability, solidarity, and empowerment, and gives teachers a voice in decisions that matter to them the most.

The important thing to remember in all four of the above methods for unifying a school's staff is that each one allows staff members a chance to give input on the things that are happening around them. The input can come in the form of dialogue, creative ideas, or physical participation. It doesn't matter what method you use to bring your staff together; as long as you allow them the opportunity to have a voice within the process, it is almost impossible to fail.

People like to have a say in the issues that affect them. To do so is very empowering and liberating. Their input gives them greater stake in the outcomes, and ties them closer to the issue at hand. The closer connection developed will foster greater participation and a willingness to take ownership of the situation and/or problem(s). Even if some of their ideas are not implemented, most people will take satisfaction in knowing their opinions were considered.

WORKING WITH TEACHERS' UNIONS

It is no secret that in most urban school districts, teachers' unions and the district administrators have an adversarial relationship. The teachers' unions often do not trust district administrators. The unions represent a segment of teaching professionals that are overworked, underpaid, and underappreciated in most urban school districts. They view the district's administrators as those who want to take away their rights, pay, and autonomy to deliver the type of instruction they believe their students will best benefit from. They believe the administrators are increasing classroom demands while neglecting to offer needed support and resources to carrying out such demands.

Most urban school administrators believe that teachers' unions often get in the way of true reform and effective change. They often point out how the teachers' contracts under the district's collective bargaining agreements make it almost impossible to get rid of an ineffective teacher and foster an attitude among teachers to give minimum effort. Administrators also complain about how easy it is for teachers to gain tenure.

They believe that once tenure is received, many teachers in urban school districts stop making an effort to improve their practice. They become stale, recycling the same material and lessons year after year, which weakens the level of instruction delivered to students.

This tumultuous relationship was created by the circumstances surrounding the majority of urban schools in this country. Urban schools are inherently different from their private, rural, and suburban school counterparts. They service higher populations of students that come from families of low socioeconomic status and poverty, and higher concentrations of students with social and emotional issues as well as multiple academic deficiencies. These students may also lack one or more of their basic fundamental needs (i.e., food, clothing, shelter, and health care).

Over the years, most urban school districts have found it difficult to recruit and retain highly qualified teaching professionals. Not only does the student population present difficulties for teachers, but many of the school buildings are badly maintained (e.g., inadequate heat and air conditioning, no running water, leaky roofs, inoperable windows, broken desks, chipped paint, and/or broken doors) and lack necessary resources (e.g., textbooks, technology, and supplies). In addition, teachers in these districts are often paid significantly less than teachers in neighboring suburban or affluent school districts.

The majority of the teaching staff in many urban school districts are less qualified or novice teachers. Highly qualified teachers either leave urban districts after a few years, or they never apply for an urban teaching position in the first place. To combat this trend, many school superintendents started to give teachers extended benefits when negotiating their contracts with unions. Since they couldn't pay teachers more money in most cases, they opted to decrease the number of years to gain tenure, decrease most of the powers held by principals, and decrease teacher responsibilities that extended outside of the classroom (just to name a few).

For example, many union contracts contain clauses that prohibit teachers from doing hall or lunchroom duty. This type of concession is problematic for building-level administrators. In some small schools, the principal may be the only administrator. Even in larger schools, the administrative staff may consist of only four people: the principal and one to three assistant principals. The school's administration can't be in all places at once. They often need teachers to step out of their classrooms between classes, and/or assist with monitoring the cafeteria.

Some teachers will assist in any manner that will benefit students, while some will refuse because they're not obligated under the contract, regardless of any benefits their actions could bring to the students or the overall success of the school. In some urban schools, some teachers are shunned by their colleagues for being too cooperative with the building's administration. This type of behavior creates tension, resentment, and animosity among teachers and principals.

The reality of the matter is that teachers need principals, and principals need teachers. The two will be forever linked together as long as there are school buildings for students to come to. Just like two people must work together to have a successful marriage and household for the betterment of their children, principals and teachers must work together for the benefit of students and the overall functioning of the school.

Since the principal is the school's leader and the person most responsible for the operation of the school building, he/she should actively work to ensure that relations between teachers and administrators remain positive. Most of the work principals do is not with the union leaders, but with the teachers themselves. Principals who are able to make teachers feel comfortable, secure, and appreciated will eliminate many of the issues that arise between unions and administrators. Some of the actions principals can do to effectively work with teachers are as follows:

• Listen to teacher concerns.
• Communicate the expectations clearly.
• Allow teachers some level of autonomy and freedom.
• Give teachers a voice in the decision-making process.
• Provide support, mentoring, feedback, and counseling.
• Create incentives and show appreciation for the work teachers do.

The above is not an exhaustive list, but a framework for showing teachers how much they are needed and valued.

Final note: one of the best ways a principal can create and maintain positive relations with teachers' unions is by placing a union representative on his/her decision-making team or cabinet. Every school building has at least one teacher who serves as a union representative for that building. Including the union representative in the decisions made about the school will give the representative a global understanding of the issues and circumstances affecting the school.

The union representative will also serve as a conduit for delivering global messages to the teaching staff, which will increase their awareness of problems and help them to understand the administrators a little better. Above all else, having the representative near the principal will help highlight what is needed to truly reform the school, and help all teachers take more ownership in the things that need to be done.

Many educators aren't as vested in their schools as they should be. Most urban school teachers don't live in the communities where the school is located, so their greatest motivation for doing the work is getting a paycheck. I'm not saying there is something wrong with educators wanting to earn an appropriate wage for the services they provide, but if that's their greatest motivation, their level of interest will not be as high as those who are connected to the school and community in more visceral ways.

If teachers can claim ownership for the things that transpire within the school, then they will take more of an active role to make things better. They will become more vested in the school's success and failure. That's the true nature of school reform and creating effective change.

EXAMPLES

Example 1: In the summer of 2005, principal Ellen Earle wanted to restructure her school building because she wanted to create better community among the teaching staff. Mrs. Earle believed that by fostering greater community, the staff's morale would improve and so would their work performance within the classroom.

Over the past three years, she noticed that the staff had become more disconnected with each passing year. They rarely had dialogues about best practices, nor did they converse with each other to simply share information. The only teachers who seemed to talk to each other were those that were in the same department. For the upcoming school year, Earle restructured the building in teams, giving common planning periods to teachers who were on the same team.

She also established school improvement committees that allowed teachers to address issues and areas they felt needed attention within the school. The new structure was well accepted by the staff. They enjoyed the time they were able to collaborate with each other, and they relished the contributions they were making to the overall improvement of the school.

Example 2: In 1999, Walker Middle School was in its last year of its school restructuring plan. If the school didn't show at least a 10 percent increase in test scores, the entire school would be reconstituted. Dr. Graham took over as principal in the same year.

On his opening day speech to his staff of 55 he stated, "Ladies and gentlemen, we are at a crossroad. We have come to a point where we must make a decision. Either we're going to stand up and fight, or we're going to lay down and die. I don't know about you, but if I have to go out, I'm going out fighting." Graham went on to say, "They want to reconstitute our school. They want to put us out of business. They think we don't have any life left in us, but they're wrong. I think we have plenty of life in us, so much so that we're going to prove it to them with improvements in this year's test scores." The crowd became very excited.

Halfway through the principal's speech, they started to applaud and cheer his every word. "Who's going to join me and stand up to the nay-sayers? Who's going to stand with me and stop those who want to cast us aside? By standing together, we can make a difference for our students!" By the end of his speech, everyone in the room was standing. The scene more resembled Sunday at a Baptist church than a staff meeting at a public school. Some of the staff members became so excited that they began shouting, "Amen! That's right! I'll stand with you! We will not let them do it to us!"

Essential Questions: Was the law followed in the above scenarios? Why or why not? If yes, what actions did the principal take to adhere to the law? If not, what should the principal have done in order to have been more effective? What did you learn from the scenarios? Would you do anything differently?

Chapter Eight

Law 8: Conduct the Critical Conversations

Urban schools in the United States, especially those located in inner cities, are in bad shape for a multitude of reasons. External factors aside, many of these schools lack functional internal structures—policies, procedures, norms, and organization. Over a period of time, the weak or nonexistent structures create disproportionate levels of inefficiency and dysfunction. Weak internal structures will topple any institution.

Inefficiency can spread through an organization faster than cancer. When structures are broken, some people will consciously (or unconsciously) exploit the situation for their own selfish gain. Others will feel helpless and frustrated because the system is not only failing them, but failing students as well. Broken structures also create a climate for staff members to become disconnected, making the functions performed by these employees unsatisfactory.

When this happens, the school could see an increase in several of the following: negative student behavioral issues, poorly maintained facilities, employees who lack effort and enthusiasm when performing job tasks, staff members who arrive to work late and/or leave early without permission, frequent misuse of property or stealing of supplies and equipment, misappropriation of funds, staff insubordination, regular acts of rudeness and/or disrespect toward visitors or students, mishandling of important documents or important duties, and/or frequently missed deadlines, just to name a few.

Principals will even encounter staff members who have convinced themselves that the little amount of work they're doing is sufficient to maintain their employment. The staff members who remain faithful and committed will eventually burn out, become frustrated, quit, or seek employment elsewhere because they're tired of carrying the bulk of the workload. They break under the pressure of carrying a disproportionate amount of responsibility with no support, reward, or gratitude.

Principals who have their fingertips on the pulse of their schools will be able to quickly find the breakdowns in the school's internal structure. What they will learn is that breakdowns in internal structures usually are caused by the actions and behaviors of the people working within those structures. A policy or procedure problem can easily be corrected, but when the problem involves people, that's an entirely different animal to tame. People issues result in the need to have the "critical conversations."

According to Patterson, Grenny, McMillan, and Switzler (2002), critical conversations (also referred to as crucial conversations) are discussions about the tough issues. The issues are tough because they are usually connected to the feelings and sensitivities of individuals being corrected. A critical conversation is the discourse that comes when confronting individuals about how their deficiencies and ineffectiveness detract from the school's achieving its larger goals. They are critical because they are the conversations that principals absolutely must have with various employees, for a multitude of reasons, throughout the course of a school year.

THE RIGHT MOTIVES

When conducting a critical conversation you must begin with the right motives and stay focused on them no matter what happens (Patterson, Grenny, McMillan, and Switzler, 2002). Principals must have a clear understanding of their motives, reasons why the conversation is necessary, and how the staff member's actions (or lack thereof) are hindering the school. The right motives are strictly about the employee's behavior and/or negligence in relation to the effectiveness of the employee's job performance.

It is the principal's duty to give his/her honest assessments about the major issues, and what should be done to resolve any and all problems. This is the time when the principal should place his/her personal feelings aside and judge the employee's performance in a pragmatic fashion. The principal's biases about the employee's character and/or personality should never enter the picture; the conversation should strictly be about the issues that play a role in the school's overall ineffectiveness.

There should also be some care as to how these types of conversations are conducted. They should always be done in a respectful manner. A principal should never talk to anyone about a controversial issue while angry or upset. Schedule a meeting in your office so that you and the staff member can sit down in an environment conducive for dialogue. Speak clearly and calmly so the person you're talking to understands your message. Make sure you stay on the topic, and don't stray or allow yourself to be led astray by the other person. Put emphasis on the undesirable action and not the person. Your goal is to get the person to acknowledge the problem, and more important, find a solution to fix the issue.

Solicit the other person's opinions and comments. Allow the other person sufficient time to speak, and find out the reasoning behind their action(s). Before concluding, try to come up with a mutual solution to the problem so there is an understanding of what the expectations are. The staff member must understand that you both have a mutual purpose for resolving any issues at hand.

TURNING POINTS, DOCUMENTATION, AND GRIEVANCES

A critical conversation could also mark the turning point in the relationship you have with the person you're dealing with. If the conversation is conducted in a nonthreatening manner, and the person is receptive to your comments and suggestions, then the issue will be resolved immediately. There will be some sincere individuals who might unknowingly make a mistake simply because no one has told them that their actions or behavior were counterproductive. They will be thankful for the feedback, and become better for it. But, if a person reverts back to his/her previous ways even after being corrected, then that person has revealed his/her true nature to you. At this point, the principal must deal with the person in an entirely different manner.

It is not uncommon for some school staff to revert back to previous negative behaviors after being confronted by the principal. This happens simply because their stagnation has got the best of them. The school has historically been a place that allowed their actions to go unchecked, without them ever having to be held accountable. Even if someone mentioned the adverse behavior to them previously, because there was no follow-up they slowly went back to their regular patterns of behavior. Some employees also revert back to their previous actions because they don't believe that anything will happen to them. They don't respect the principal's authority, and they believe that by virtue of their length of employment, or the status they've acquired from their peers, they can operate with impunity.

The principal must take quick action when this happens, and not allow the issue(s) to fester and become worse. The first thing you must do is document everything. Every time you have a conversation with the employee, follow it up with a memo outlining the conversation. The memo should contain the date, purpose of the conversation, what was discussed, and the expected outcome(s). Present a copy of the memo to the staff member for their records. It is also good to request that the employee sign the memo. The documentation will later serve as your evidence that shows how you tried to assist the employee and/or correct the negative action.

Second, you should have a good understanding of the employee's contract under the district's collective bargaining agreement (if applicable). If the teaching staff follows one contract and the support staff another, then the principal should become familiar with both. The contracts will outline how principals should move through the disciplinary process for particular employees. It will also protect principals from grievances and claims of harassment.

Many principals make huge mistakes in this area. They might have an employee on their staff who is negligent in his/her duties and responsibilities, but principals go about correcting the behavior in the wrong way. Instead of going through the proper procedures, they immediately try to jump to suspension or possible termination, or they get into a verbal altercation with the employee and never document the incident at all.

Other times when these situations occur, the employee files grievances against the principal for violation of rights and/or not following the disciplinary process accurately. If the matter ever makes it to litigation status, the principal will lose every time if he/she didn't follow the details of the employee's contract, or follow proper protocol.

In any grievance hearing, the first thing that will be checked is whether or not the principal violated any rights of the employee. If the principal didn't adhere to the procedures outlined in the union contract, then the employee's rights were violated—according to the judge. Once it has been determined that the employee's rights were violated, then that will become the glaring issue, not the quality of the employee's performance. Once that can of worms is opened, almost any future complaints about the employee's performance could be twisted into harassment charges on behalf of the employee.

Many labor union contracts have made it almost impossible to get rid of an inadequate employee. This is why adhering to the contract is so important for principals. It will take you through the chains of protocol: verbal warning, written reprimand, professional development plans, suspension, and/or termination of employment (which is typical in most union contracts). If the employee's behavior doesn't change, the contract will serve as your most important weapon.

One final note about critical conversations: they are going to get under some people's skin no matter how delicately you deliver your message. The education profession is very emotionally charged. Some may even perceive your words during a critical conversation as a personal attack against them, which may be far from what you intended.

In many urban school districts across the country, the relationship between the administration and the teachers' unions have become increasingly adversarial. In some districts, the relationship is so tense that any attempt at positive change on behalf of the principal (or the district's central office administrative staff) is viewed through a cynical lens. The purpose for having a critical conversation with an employee is to bring the adverse behaviors affecting the school to the forefront so that they can be corrected. Principals can't afford to sacrifice the greater needs of the school for the sake of saving the sensitive feelings of someone who is not doing a good job in his/her position.

This is one of the most crucial areas of school leadership that will test the principal's mettle. This is the point where many principals fall short. Far too often, principals in urban schools want to play nice, or to be viewed as the "good guy/gal." They want to get along with everyone in an effort to be liked or to avoid causing any waves. They believe that being liked by everyone will lead to job security. They also want to try to avoid the potential conflict that could come out of such conversations.

The truth is, you can't be all things to all people. Some of the people principals encounter will not have the school's best interests at heart. Why would you want to be liked by them? In fact, anyone who stands in the way of your school's success should be considered your professional enemy. True reform and inefficient practices can't coexist within a school if the school has any chance of ever achieving success. If principals want effective changes within their schools, they must not be afraid to ruffle feathers and to shake things up when necessary. Having critical conversations with your staff will definitely lend itself to doing such.

Leadership is not an easy task; if it were, everyone would be a leader. The best way to obtain real job security in an urban school district is by creating positive reforms that will improve the school. Conversations with people about their performance, or lack thereof, is a major component of the school's reformation process. Principals who avoid critical conversations are contributing to their own failure.

EXAMPLE

Mr. Pringle has been the principal of his high school for five years. He hired Mr. Wright at the beginning of his fifth year to fill a vacant social studies position. On the fourth day of school, Pringle walked into Wright's class for one of his usual walk-ins. Walk-ins usually last 10–15 minutes. This time it was extended because when Pringle came into the classroom, he saw Wright sitting behind his desk reading a magazine. There were 11 students in the class (five girls and six boys). Three of the girls were in a corner combing each other's hair. Four students were on cell phones (one was having a conversation while the other three appeared to be playing games or texting).

Two male students had a heated debate about which NFL team was going to win the Super Bowl, one student listened to an iPod, and one student slept. Pringle was heated. It angered him to see the students' educational time wasted, but he held his composure and sat in the class for the last 35 minutes to see if Wright was going to deliver any instruction. He never did.

When the class ended, Pringle asked Wright why he didn't attempt to teach a lesson. Wright responded by saying, "I tried to teach them before you walked in, but these kids don't value their education. They wouldn't listen to me, so I left them to their devices." Pringle left the classroom and immediately went to his office to jot down what he saw in the classroom and Wright's comments.

After school Pringle called Wright down to his office to discuss what he saw. During the meeting, all Wright stated was, "The kids don't want to learn. They won't listen." Pringle went over some strategies for Wright to use in his classroom, and gave him a deadline for implementing the strategies. He also explained to Wright that allowing students to do whatever they wanted was not an option. Wright seemed very receptive to the suggestions and said he would implement them immediately. Pringle also typed up the things they discussed in a letter and gave Wright a copy before he left.

Over the span of five weeks, five separate incidents happened. First, a female student burst into the office in tears during third period. She said a male student poked her in her "private area" with an umbrella.

When the principal asked the student what the teacher did, the student said he didn't do anything; she started crying not because of what the other student did, but because the teacher didn't try to assist her or reprimand the student who violated her. She said Mr. Wright stated to her, "Well, if you didn't wear your pants so tight, the boys probably wouldn't pick on you."

Second, students started throwing books out the window during Wright's last period class. One of the books hit a parent as she was walking into the building. Third, Wright's entire fourth period class decided to leave the classroom and go to the cafeteria for what would be their second lunch. Wright never attempted to stop the students nor did he report that students left his room without permission.

Last, there were two fights involving students. One took place during his fifth period class, while the other took place in the hall. A student who should have been in Wright's class left without permission and punched an unsuspecting student in the hallway.

All of the incidents were documented by Pringle. He also followed the progressive disciplinary procedures written in the teachers' union contract that governed teacher behavior and responsibilities. Due to the number of incidents, and the number of times Wright was written up, Wright was placed on an intervention contract. The contract outlined the classroom issues associated with Wright, and actions he should take to resolve them. The intervention contract had an expiration date of 90 days. At the end of the time noted on the contract, a hearing would be held to determine whether Wright would be able to keep his employment.

Ten days into the intervention contract, Wright's sixth period class locked him out of the classroom. One of the assistant principals had to open the door to let Wright back in because he didn't have his keys. Fifteen days into the intervention plan, Pringle came back into his class to do a walk-in and discovered a scene similar to his initial walk-in during the first week of school. Wright sat behind his desk while the students did nothing. When the principal saw this, he politely asked Wright to step outside. Wright declined. Pringle asked him a second time, then Wright erupted in a fit of rage in front of the students, "No! I will not go outside with you. I'm tired of you harassing me. You call me down to your office all the time about this and that. I'm getting sick of it! Leave me alone! Either you're going to allow me to conduct my class the way I see fit, or I'm going to file a grievance against you!"

Pringle held his composure and left the classroom. He went to his office and contacted two people: the assistant superintendent (his supervisor) and the teachers' union's building representative. Pringle not only rehashed the current incident, but he also informed them of all recent incidents since Wright had been placed on the intervention plan.

One week later, a meeting was held concerning Wright's status of employment. It was determined that Wright was willfully neglecting his duties and was unable to perform the responsibilities required despite assistance from the school's administration. Pringle provided a binder filled with various forms of documentation (emails, reprimands, conferences, peer collaborations meetings, teacher mentor notes, suggested professional development sessions, etc.). Wright was terminated effective immediately.

Essential Questions: Was the law followed in the above scenario? Why or why not? If yes, what actions did the principal take to adhere to the law? If not, what should the principal have done in order to have been more effective? What did you learn from the scenario? Would you do anything differently?

Chapter Nine

Law 9: Learn to Delegate

Many principals are able to get things done in their schools by sheer will-power. Due to the high stakes involved with the urban school principalship, some holding the position will literally try to handle many of the important functions by themselves. They put the weight of their schools on their backs and try to move forward by their own unrelenting drive and determination.

It is not uncommon to find principals in urban schools performing duties that cross multiple positions (i.e., secretarial, janitorial, managerial, instructional, and/or counseling). Most principals in urban schools think it's their duty as the head administrator to consistently pick up the slack when others fail to do so. This thinking is as false as it is common.

When principals do the work of others within the school, they indirectly send the message that they don't trust the abilities of the people who should be doing the tasks, or that staff members are ineffective. Principals who do this are also displaying to everyone that they don't completely understand their role as principal and leader of the school building.

It is the principal's job to administer, and that's exactly what he/she should do. Principals should never attempt to perform the duties of others. Effective administrators do not try to play a direct role in the day-to-day lives of their employees (Marzano, 2003). They let their employees perform their duties while observing, monitoring, and providing assistance and support when needed.

Principals who are guilty of such actions think they are merely doing what needs to be done, multitasking or modeling the correct way to do things; but that is not the reality. When principals behave in this manner, they are actually supporting the inappropriate, inefficient, and/or negligent actions of their employees. By doing the work for them, you're telling personnel that they're not accountable and don't have to meet standards or improve their practices. This kind of action on the principal's behalf reinforces a pattern of behavior that is detrimental to the school's overall performance and overall functioning.

It will also diminish the principal's authority in the eyes of other employees. As the chief administrator, the essence of your job is to lead, oversee, manage, govern, facilitate, support, coach, and guide others. Stepping outside of this too often will lead to a loss of respect and authority you need in order to get things done in a timely fashion. If you are going to do most of the secretary's responsibilities, for example, then you don't need an extra person occupying that particular position; the same holds true for any position in the school building.

In many urban schools, there are individuals in various positions throughout the school building who are getting paid to do nothing. These folks have been able to linger around and feed off the school year after year—becoming complacent and stagnant in their own do-nothingness. Failure to hold every individual on the school's staff accountable fosters a culture of inefficiency and ineffectiveness. The principal's job is challenging enough without adding on the duties others are being paid to perform. You must refrain from becoming bogged down in the duties/details of others within the school building.

It is very foolish for principals to think they can operate a school by themselves. Trying to do it all yourself is not only unrealistic, but it is the fastest way down the road toward burnout and early retirement. Furthermore, in order to lead a school, especially one with a history of failure, principals need clarity. They need to be able to see the big picture in order to make the best decisions for the school, its stakeholders, and its interconnected parts. This type of clarity cannot be obtained if the principal is inundated with duties or tasks that someone else should be performing. It's good for the principal to know the intricate details of other positions in the school, but it is not his/her place to actually do them.

It is your place as the principal to build capability within your school so that others feel empowered, encouraged, and confident enough to do their jobs (and other tasks needed) successfully. The only way to do this is by having people trained properly, and by delegating. According to Marzano (2003), effective principals engage in behaviors that focus on the efficient running of the school, but they are not intrusive in the daily routines and practices (although effective principals do communicate an interest in these routines and practices).

Let's analyze the game of baseball for example. The way this game is played closely parallels how a school operates. In baseball, you have a lot of players who are specialists in the functions they perform (catcher, pitcher, first through third basemen, shortstop, and the outfielders). There is also a team manager who sits in the dugout while the game is being played. He observes his players actions and monitors their performance.

The team manager also provides leadership, coaching, and tutelage to his players so they'll be able to perform at a high level during the game, which will give them the best chance of winning. If a player doesn't perform well after assistance has been provided, the manager makes substitutions. The managers rarely come out on the field because they do not have a position to play on the field. On the rare occasions when a manager decides to leave the dugout and go on the field, the game stops and there is usually confusion and turmoil on the field until the manager goes back to where he belongs.

A school operates in a similar way because it too requires specialists (teachers, custodians, aides, secretaries, psychologists, counselors, security guards, coaches, business managers, registrars, assistant principals, etc.). The principal's duties mirror that of the baseball team's manager. It's a position that's performed best from the sidelines. This is how you'll be able to study the game (how the school operates) and observe the big picture. You'll never see the team manager of a baseball team leave the dugout and start pitching, catching, or throwing balls during the game. That's not his place, nor is it the principal's place to start doing tasks not suited to the position.

In the game of education, training employees properly and delegating is the only way to be effective. Most school employees have to complete specialized training and/or acquire certifications as part of their conditions of employment. Allow them to do what they were trained to do, and get out of the way. Principals need to be able to observe things holistically. They need to observe what's going on in real time, just like a baseball manager.

Delegating will also help to identify those who can, and who can't, perform adequately. Knowing this information will either direct you toward helping that person become successful in their duties, or motivate you to find a replacement. There are many tasks in the school that are exclusive to the principal. Stick to those tasks, do them well, and delegate the rest. This will build confidence in your staff and help the school run more efficiently.

EXAMPLE

Mrs. Williams has been a middle school principal at the same school for four years. When she first arrived at the school, she inherited a staff of fifty-five with an average of ten years of employment within the school. During her first two years as principal, she found herself staying five to six hours extra after school each day because she was doing tasks that should have been assigned to others.

Many of the schools employees didn't do their jobs correctly or they were often absent. She also experienced multiple incidents of tasks botched up after being assigned to certain people, because they didn't follow her directions correctly. Since Williams didn't trust these employees for even simple tasks, she would do them herself or assign the extra duties to one of the few people she did trust. The peculiar part about this problem is that when it was time to do the yearly evaluations of these employees, she rated them as satisfactory.

At the end of Williams's second year, she made a vow that she would do things differently. She would stop doing the tasks of others and hold them accountable by directly linking their performance (no matter how good or bad) to their annual evaluations. She began using her new approach with Mr. Butler, her assistant principal. She assigned Butler the task of completing the school emergency evacuation plan.

This task was assigned to Butler during the previous year, but Williams took it over during the last week before it was due because Butler wasn't on pace to finish it on time. Butler had three weeks to complete the task due to the complexity of the document. He was well liked by everyone in the school. He was funny, had a good personality, and had a good rapport with students and parents. Williams took over the task and worked on it day and night until it was done.

When Williams assigned it to Butler the second time, she again gave him three weeks to complete it and told him to see her if he should have any questions. At the end of the first week, Williams checked with Butler on the status of the emergency plan, and to see if he needed any assistance. Butler assured her that he was okay and that he would have the plan completed on time.

Williams checked with him again at the end of the second week, and again, he assured her that the plan would be completed on time. Williams asked to see the first ten pages of the plan, but Butler claimed he left it at home on the hard drive of his home computer, and would bring it in the following day. The next day, Butler told Williams he saved the document to his flash drive, but accidentally left his flash drive at home on his kitchen table. Butler again reassured her that he had the materials and that he would have the plan completed on time.

Williams was a little worried that Butler wasn't going to come through, like the previous year. She started to help him out by working with him to complete the plan like she did the previous year, but then she decided not to do it. She wanted to see if Butler was going to deliver as he promised. On the day the plan was due, Butler came into Williams's office with only five pages of the 25 page document.

The five pages that he did have were incomplete and unorganized. Williams said, "This is unacceptable work, Mr. Butler. You had three weeks to complete this and I asked you repeatedly if you needed any help. This was an important document that's being requested from central office, and you treated it as if it had no importance. You told me that you would have this completed and it isn't. So what's the problem? Why isn't it done?"

Butler responded by saying, "Well, I was going to do it but I was busy with student discipline and dealing with irate parents. The past few weeks have been rough. Things can get out of control here at times. I just couldn't get around to it. You know how it is."

Before dismissing Butler, Williams informed Butler that she was going to document this incident and it would be added to his midyear evaluation. She also informed him that the next time he doesn't complete an assigned task without informing her in advance, it will result in him being written up for willful neglect of duty. After the meeting with Butler was over, Williams called the central office staff person who requested the plan and asked for a three-day extension. The extension was granted. Williams gathered her documents from last year's emergency plan and created a new document and submitted it.

Throughout the course of the year, Butler had other tasks that he either did incorrectly or not at all. At the end of the year, Williams gave Butler a poor evaluation and requested his immediate transfer. Her request was granted.

Essential Questions: Was the law followed in the above scenario? Why or why not? If yes, what actions did the principal take to adhere to the law? If not, what should the principal have done in order to have been more effective? What did you learn from the scenario? Would you do anything differently?

Chapter Ten

Law 10: Don't Attempt to Change Too Much Too Soon

One boring day while at home, I decided to see if there was anything good on television. While channel surfing, I landed on one of the science stations. A scientist was conducting some sort of experiment using live tadpoles. The scientist discovered that when a tadpole is dropped into water with an unfavorable temperature (too hot or too cold), it will automatically try to jump out. But when the same tadpole is dropped into water with a temperature it finds favorable, it will stay in that water.

Next, the tadpole was placed in a beaker of water with a mild temperature, which was set on a hot burner. While the tadpole was on the burner, the scientist gradually increased the heat. This was done to see if the tadpole would jump out of the beaker of water once the water became uncomfortable. The scientist observed that even after the heat was turned up on the burner, and the water began to boil, the tadpole would not leap out of the beaker—not even to save its own life.

I didn't catch the beginning of the program, so I don't know why a scientist was trying to cook a tadpole on television, but the part that I did see really taught me a lesson about change, and made me think about how people within urban schools deal with this phenomenon. Change is very peculiar in a sense that people can see or feel the need for change, know that it's inevitable, but will resist it in order to remain in their comfortable/stagnant state of existence.

The tadpole in the above example reminds me of how many employees in urban schools behave. The tadpole would not jump out of the water, not even to save its own life, even though the heated water reached temperatures that would have killed it. It refused to change. Many staff members in urban schools behave in the same way. They feel the heat from the deterioration of the school, but they will elect to remain there and not take a different course of action to save themselves or the school.

Change seems to cause a paralyzing fear in people, making it difficult for them to take appropriate action. Many people say they love and embrace change, but not all of them are telling the truth. Principals will encounter staff members, students, parents, and other stakeholders who will complain about the problems of the school, but as soon as the principals start to reform the issues people complain about, some of those same people will become upset and resistant. In essence, what they're saying is they want change, but they just don't want to make any changes themselves. That's an oxymoron of the highest degree.

This is why principals should not attempt to change too much in a school too soon; no matter what condition the school is in, it didn't get in this state overnight, so principals shouldn't take a microwaveable approach to school reform. Change should be gradual. Too much change in a short amount of time will make people fearful, nervous, and uncomfortable. They become this way because the changes will affect their comfort levels.

For some people, being comfortable in a bad situation is more tolerable than the transformation process because it will take some sacrifice on their behalf in order to transition to a higher plane. Their greatest fear is the unknown, so they would rather remain where they are. Even though it's not an ideal state of existence, at least they are familiar with it. This is how many urban school employees rationalize their state within the school, and the state of the school itself.

There are two approaches urban school principals can follow in order to adhere to Law 10. First, principals can make small, gradual changes each year, until the cumulative changes add up to major reforms. Small changes are ones like cosmetic changing to the building, reorganizing book distribution and supplies, and reestablishing school pride—just to name a few. Every school building is different, so the small changes would be particular to each school.

The second approach is to target one major issue at a time, and stay on said issue until the issue has been resolved. This means taking on one gross dysfunction or inefficient practice at a time. The major issues are also particular to each school, but some major issues that are common in most urban schools are improving student discipline (classroom behavior, suspensions, and expulsions), increasing graduation rates, aligning instructional practices with state standards, improving staff morale, and attaining more parental engagement and involvement.

The main idea with the second approach is that by tackling one major issue at a time, many of the smaller items will be resolved in the process. Understand that most major issues are major because they have been able to grow and develop over a prolonged period of time. So when principals take on these types of issues, they must know that the issues will not be resolved overnight—it will take time and persistence. How much time depends on the mentality of the principal handling the issue, the competence of the staff that the principal has at his/her disposal, and the types of major issues affecting the school. Principals must attack major school issues strategically and persistently until the problem is resolved.

EXAMPLE

Michael Freeman took leadership of a high school that had a bad reputation for student violence. Two years before he became principal, a fifteen-year-old student shot and killed a seventeen-year-old student inside the boys' restroom. One year before Freeman arrived, there was an all-out riot during one of the football games. The incident made the local news. The parents of two students got into a fight, which led to the mayhem. Twelve people were injured and thirty arrests were made (seventeen of those arrested were adults and the rest were students).

Upon becoming principal, Freeman wanted to change the school's environment by making it safe. The first thing he did was hire more security guards. He also restricted access to the school building, permanently locking many of the school's doors that didn't have a metal detector in front of them. Each student and staff member was required to have identification cards with a picture attached. He also connected with a local grassroots organization that cosponsored Stop the Violence programs. Many of the sponsored events took place at the school.

The changes were much needed and made the school a lot safer and more orderly. After the first five months of school, there were no instances of violence. Most of the staff members were pleased with the changes, but there were a few teachers who were upset because they had to enter the building from the front instead of the side door next to the parking lot. But for the most part, Freeman was the darling of the staff and community.

Starting in his second year as principal, Freeman introduced a host of new changes. For example, shortly before the winter break, Freeman started to notice many teachers decorating their classroom doors with Christmas decorations. He also noticed that many teachers were preparing for what was the annual Christmas program. The yearly Christmas assembly started years ago with Mrs. Johnson, the school's art teacher.

Johnson had been a teacher in the building for 13 years. The Christmas program was a side project that she organized. It was typically used as a morale booster for both staff and students. Everyone looked forward to it each year. Two weeks before the winter break, Freeman called a staff meeting after school. He passed out copied pages from his school law book. One of the pages he highlighted contained portions that prohibited the promotion of religious holidays within the school setting. He also stated that religious holidays must be taught in a secular manner, pointing out instances where the school staff had violated the state laws concerning this issue.

Freeman demanded that all the door decorations come down and all curriculum materials and lessons be submitted to him before administered to the student body. He also told Johnson that the Christmas assembly would be canceled unless she changed the format to make it more secular (including all religious celebrations during the season). Johnson, and some others, protested.

They informed Freeman that the Christmas program was a school tradition and must be left as it is. Freeman disagreed, referring back to the highlighted portions he copied for them from the school law book. The staff was very upset, but they complied because the law was plain and clear.

Freeman didn't stop there. He inserted a host of other changes soon after. He put a new code on the copier so that only office staff had access to it— arguing that too much money was being spent out of the school's budget on copy paper. He also changed the way teachers could access materials and supplies, required teachers to submit weekly lesson plans every Friday before leaving, and changed many of the locks on various doors in the school—only giving master keys to the custodians and the administrative staff.

Many teachers, and other staff members, began to resent Freeman. They talked behind his back and criticized his every move. They would smile and be cordial, but deep down inside most of his staff didn't approve of the rapid changes, no matter how necessary they might have been. Because of this, staff morale was very low. Many teachers deliberately took days off, especially during some of the most critical times (e.g., the state standardized testing week).

One day, Freeman saw Mrs. Jackson walking in his direction down the hall. He noticed her outfit because it was color coordinated nicely; her hat, belt, earrings, and shoes were the same color. As the two of them crossed paths, Freeman stated, "Good day, Mrs. Jackson. You look lovely today."

Jackson smiled and continued to walk into her classroom, while Freeman went to check on a matter in the cafeteria. Later that same day, Freeman found out from his secretary that Jackson left work early today. He remembered seeing her in the hall in passing, but she didn't appear to be ill. The secretary went on to say that Jackson wanted her to let him know that he would be hearing from her lawyer.

Freeman was very confused to say the least. He wanted to know not only why Jackson left early, but also why she made such a threat. Jackson didn't report to work the following day either. Freeman tried calling her home but was unsuccessful at reaching her. By the end of the day, Freeman received an urgent fax from central office.

Jackson filed a complaint against Freeman claiming sexual harassment. Moments later, Freeman received a call from his direct supervisor wanting to get his side of the story. His supervisor also stated that Jackson could be filing criminal charges against him and could possibly go to the media. Freeman was also advised to contact his attorney for counsel. Freeman was stunned. He didn't know how a simple comment could have been blown so far out of proportion.

The incident made the local newspaper, which made Freeman very angry. He felt that his reputation was being greatly damaged over nothing. From that point on, he became very defensive and leery of his staff. He stopped smiling and he wouldn't speak to anyone unless he had to. Jackson eventually dropped all charges against him, but he was already hurt emotionally and professionally. He served in his position as principal for another year after the scandal, but he didn't come back for a third year. He moved out of the city and found work in another school district.

Essential Questions: Was the law followed in the above scenario? Why or why not? If yes, what actions did the principal take to adhere to the law? If not, what should the principal have done in order to have been more effective? What did you learn from the scenario? Would you do anything differently?

Chapter Eleven

Law 11: Determine What Good Instruction Looks Like

Pick any troubled urban school anywhere in America and spend a little time visiting various classrooms for one day. What you will find is that there is no continuity, consistency, or interconnectedness in regard to instructional implementation, delivery, and practice. Some teachers in urban schools rely too heavily on lecturing, direct instruction, textbook assignments (read the chapter and answer the questions), videos unrelated to the subject, note taking, and/or copying.

In a short amount of time, their lessons become stale, uninteresting to students, and unsuited for boosting achievement—which results in poor student performance and increased student behavioral issues. This is more than just a problem; it's more like an issue that has reached epidemic proportions. I would be the first to admit that there are a lot of great teachers who work in urban schools. These teachers do an outstanding job each day—going above and beyond the call of duty to create exciting and engaging lessons for students on a daily basis—but unfortunately, these teachers seem to be few and far between in a lot of schools.

In the movie *Forrest Gump,* the character Forrest stated the unforgettable line, "Life is like a box of chocolates. You just never know what you're going to get." One can say the same thing about the types, and levels, of classroom instruction that take place in some urban schools—you just never know what you're going to get. In one classroom you will find organization, efficiency, and productivity. But in the classroom directly across the hall, one will see the exact opposite. The inconsistencies are a result of teachers not having a solid understanding of what good instruction is, and what it looks like in action.

It is no secret that many of the issues that currently plague urban schools deter many of the best and brightest teachers from applying to urban school districts. They would rather work in conditions that are more suitable, where there are fewer student behavioral issues and academic barriers, and more support and resources. Unless a teacher with outstanding qualities makes a conscious effort to work with the most challenging populations, urban schools are generally left with hiring the inexperienced and unsuspecting (teachers who don't have a clue about the challenges they'll face). This translates into urban school teaching positions not being filled with the best possible candidates.

This would explain the caliber of work being given to urban students, and the types of instruction being delivered. Many teachers who lecture and assign "busy work" to students every day for nine months truly believe they're doing a good job, and are delivering quality lessons to students. Each teacher has his/her own varied opinions about what good instruction looks like.

It is part of the principal's job to establish what good instruction is, and define what it looks like in action; that is, creating the school's own "brand" of educating students. Creating your own brand of instructional delivery doesn't mean that teachers have to use prescribed words and lesson, or operate in a robotlike fashion. It simply means that teachers are aware of the instructional goals, and they're all willing to incorporate common practices to accomplish those goals.

For example, there are a lot of pizzerias in the United States, but there are very few pizzas that taste the same. Pizza is nothing more than bread, tomato sauce, cheese, and a few toppings; but each establishment does it differently to give it its own distinctiveness, or brand. The same should also hold true for schools. We're essentially dealing with educating students (teaching and learning), but each school needs to make sure its distinctiveness is carried out in the way instruction is delivered to students, and it is the principal's job to ensure that this happens in every classroom. Principals can establish how instruction should be delivered in their schools by using the following mechanisms.

CREATE INTERESTING PROFESSIONAL DEVELOPMENT SESSIONS

Principals can establish and maintain effective instructional delivery and practices through the use of professional development and training sessions. Professional development is the platform principals can use to create instructional cohesiveness. This is the time when instructional norms, goals, and expectations can be established.

If teachers know what is expected of them instructionally, then they'll be better able to meet those expectations. If the expectation is for each teacher to begin class with a warm-up question, and end it with a closing assignment or recap, then it should be explained and/or demonstrated during the teachers' development sessions and trainings. If teachers are expected to check students' understanding before moving on to a new concept, then that too should be reflected during the teachers' professional development.

Professional development is commonly an area of neglect for most urban schools. Most urban schools do not have additional funds to hire outside professional development consultants to come to the school and conduct workshops. This forces principals to hold only the mandatory sessions dictated by central office, but in some cases there is very little development experienced by the staff, if any at all. Professional development should be something that's part of the school's culture, and carried out on a regular and consistent basis.

Please note that the professional development sessions for the teaching staff should match the instructional needs of the school. For example, if the teaching staff has issues associated with differentiated instruction, effective use of time, and/or creating common assessments, then the professional development sessions should be geared to address those issues. Far too often, principals let central office personnel dictate their professional development topics. To do so is a very big mistake. The people in central office are not in the schools regularly (in some cases not at all), and therefore they don't know the unique instructional needs of the staff.

Central office staff do have access to data that's germane to all schools in the district, so following their training schedule for some topics could be beneficial, but principals should deviate and implement sessions that directly connect with the issues affecting teachers at their schools. Principals have to decide what is important and prioritize, even if it means doing the opposite of what central office suggests.

MODELING GOOD INSTRUCTION FOR TEACHERS

The principal is not only a manager, supervisor, coach, and mentor, but also an instructional leader. A person who holds such a position should consider himself a teacher of teachers. This means a principal should be able to deliver the same level of instruction to teachers during professional development that he/she wants delivered to students. This is the true definition of modeling.

Modeling good instruction is the best way to send a clear message to the teaching staff about how instruction should take place within the classrooms. It is a very powerful tool because teachers get to visually see good instruction in action. Many principals who work in urban schools do not model instruction for teachers simply because they're not instructionally sound themselves.

Go into any urban school during one of the school's professional development sessions. You'll probably see a lot of lecturing, slides, and more lecturing. After about fifteen minutes, the principal has lost half of the audience. After thirty minutes most, if not all, of the staff are hearing words, but none of the information being presented is sinking in. After an hour, people are not even pretending to pay attention any more. Sidebar conversations start taking place, teachers will start grading papers, or they will frequently leave the room for "restroom breaks." I find it very ironic that most principals evaluate teachers and hold them to teaching standards that they can't perform themselves.

Most professional development sessions conducted in urban schools are boring, dull, and lifeless, which mirrors the types of instruction delivered to students. Many school principals do not plan their development sessions thoroughly. They merely regurgitate the scripts and materials delivered down to them from central office—making their presentations inauthentic. If the principal's professional development sessions were evaluated with the same level of scrutiny as a teacher's classroom instruction, most principals would probably fail miserably.

Principals must provide development that is useful, relevant, and engaging for teachers. When students are engaged and learning, they respond accordingly. Likewise, if teachers believe they're getting something useful during the development sessions, principals will see a difference in their staffs' attitudes toward professional development, and they too will respond accordingly. Understand that principals who can't demonstrate sound instructional practices can't rightfully expect their teachers to do the same for students.

EFFECTIVE EVALUATION

Effective evaluation is just as critical as the two previous components with regard to establishing consistently good instructional practices throughout the school building. No matter how good an instructional leader a principal is, there are going to be some teachers who will participate in the development sessions, but will go back to doing the same thing they're used to doing out of habit and routine. They will not try to employ any of the strategies delivered to them no matter how useful the strategies might be, or how they pertain to the topics the teacher is presenting. In most schools, this segment of the teaching population is small, but if you work in an urban school with a history of failure and low performance, this segment of the teaching population could be rather large.

These teachers behave this way because of stagnation and denial. When the principal speaks of change and how things will be different, they don't really believe it. If they've been in the building long enough, they've probably experienced other principals who previously spoke the same language of change, but nothing happened. They've become complacent within their environment to the point where they've given up. They've stopped believing that effective change can take place and that things within the school can get better.

Complacency is a normal human response that happens when we become too comfortable with our surroundings. We get used to the routines, norms, and predictable nature of the people and stimuli around us. When an environment becomes too comfortable, some people lose their drive and their thinking capacity diminishes. They cease to have those epiphanies or "aha!" moments that transform brilliant ideas into reality, and make real teaching and learning possible. People who become stagnant will stay in this dormant state until something threatens their existence and/or their environment, forcing them to make the necessary changes for their survival.

I've seen the debilitating effects of stagnation in many different schools, and many different areas of life and society as well. Let's briefly look at the institution of marriage for example. I've seen women do a total transformation of the worst sort after a few years of being in a comfortable marriage. When they were dating and being courted by their future husbands they dressed attractively, made regular trips to the beauty parlor, wore alluring perfumes and makeup, watched their diet, and so on. A few years later stagnation has set in; they've gained a lot of weight, stopped caring about their appearance, and their attitude for excitement has diminished.

On the flip side, there are men who suffer from the same disease. In the beginning of their relationships they were spontaneous, fun, and charming. After a few years of being in a comfortable marriage, they stop doing the things that made them appealing to their mate. When the relationship goes sour, the stagnant person will sit around scratching his/her head trying to figure out what went wrong.

Teachers in many of America's failing urban schools are no different from the types of people described in the above examples; in fact, some of them are the same people I mentioned in the examples above. Some teachers become comfortable in their job stability, unions, tenure, or they fall prey to the false notion that they're irreplaceable—knowing that there aren't an abundance of teachers clamoring for their positions. Unless something challenges their false sense of stability and comfort, nothing will change. One of the best and most expedient ways to move someone out of stagnation is to rattle their foundation. This means threatening the source of their comfort.

For urban school employees, the source of their comfort is their job security. This may sound harsh, and might go against anything one might read in another school leadership reform book, but it's the honest truth. The only language stale individuals understand is one that threatens their comfort zone. This is done by the effective use of the district's evaluation tool.

In order to get consistency in every classroom, principals must hold each teacher accountable to those tenets delivered during the professional development sessions by linking these to the teachers' yearly evaluations. For example, if your professional development sessions were centered around standard-based instruction, teaching to multiple learning styles, classroom management, and/or varying classroom instructional activities, then those components should be a heavily weighted piece of the evaluation process.

When stagnant teachers start seeing their evaluation scores drop, they will begin to take notice. They will begin to pay more attention and implement whatever is needed. Low scores equate to ineffectiveness. Ineffectiveness equates to a loss of job security, which will lead to termination of employment if the low performance continues.

Remember that evaluating teachers according to the instructional practices set forth by the school's administration not only holds teachers accountable, but it also creates consistency and continuity regarding how instruction is delivered to students. Just like companies such as Nike, Coca-Cola, McDonald's, Kentucky Fried Chicken, Burger King, Starbucks, and Levi's, schools must establish their own "brand" of instruction that is recognizable in every classroom, and with every teacher.

EXAMPLE

"We've done a lot of work around improving our instructional practices," stated Carter Johnson, principal of a college preparatory academy located in southwestern Ohio. "When visiting our classrooms, you will find the standards and objectives posted in every classroom, along with an agenda outlining the day's activities.

"We not only post them, but our teachers review them with students to make sure that they are aware of what's expected of them each day. Our school has also adopted the constructivist paradigm as our foundation for delivering instruction. We adopt this philosophy for our school out of the need to engage students better than what we were doing."

Johnson had too many teachers that would stand in front of the class with their overhead projector, or they would do all of the talking while students sat passively in their seats. With constructivism, teachers act more as facilitators. Students are doing most of the talking now because they're working in groups, making presentations, collaborating on projects, and researching the information themselves.

When asked about resistance to the school's newly adopted practices, here's what Johnson had to say: "There was some resistance in the beginning. There were some members of our staff who didn't want to change. They saw the constructivist approach as them giving up control over their classroom. They felt threatened by having students converse with each other, and by moving around in the classroom. They thought it would lead to classroom management problems.

"Despite the resistance, we keep going with it—including it in all of our professional development meetings. Some teachers even became upset with me when they received low scores on their evaluations. Before I became principal of the school, some of the teachers received very high evaluation scores, despite the school's low student achievement. I was puzzled to find that over 80 percent of the staff had perfect evaluation scores, but we barely made the continuous improvement category on the state report card.

"They were set in their ways, but fortunately for us, those teachers are no longer here. Some resigned and a few transferred to other buildings for fear of being terminated. Now we have a group of teachers who have bought into the philosophy and it's making a difference in the way we're educating our students. Instead of having students falling asleep in class, or passively disengaged, we now have students who are active participants in their learning. They're raising their hands, asking questions, and discussing the information."

Essential Questions: Was the law followed in the above scenario? Why or why not? If yes, what actions did the principal take to adhere to the law? If not, what should the principal have done in order to have been more effective? What did you learn from the scenario? Would you do anything differently?

Chapter Twelve

Law 12: Create a Strategic Plan for Improving Student Discipline and Staff Morale

If one were to rate the 12 laws in this book in order of importance, this law could arguably be listed in the top two or three. Teacher morale and student discipline are the two essentials of most urban/inner-city schools. Low teacher morale leads to high absenteeism, low self-efficacy, and low student achievement.

Schools with a history of low morale have a difficult time attracting and maintaining good teachers. A lack of control over student discipline leads to increased suspensions, low student achievement, and a bad school reputation (just to name a few). Parents will not feel comfortable sending their children to schools with a high volume of student behavioral issues. Before I discuss how to implement this law, let's first look at reasons why teacher morale and student discipline have become such huge problems for urban/inner-city schools.

TEACHER MORALE: WHY IS IT SO LOW?

There are three main reasons why teacher morale is so low in urban schools: increased workload and responsibility, lack of support from administrators, and increased student discipline issues. If we look at some of the trends in education, one of the most glaring is that teachers are being asked to do more with less. They're also being asked to come in earlier and stay later, without being financially compensated in most cases.

The issues are compounded for teachers who work in urban schools because many of their students do not get their basic psychological, emotional, social, and physical needs met. Many teachers who work in urban/inner-city schools not only have to play the role of teacher, but in some cases they're being asked to play parent, counselor, social worker, mentor, and disciplinarian. It seems that many of the breakdowns in society, and the issues that used to fall under parenting, are now being thrown at schools to fix. The increased responsibilities eventually lead to burnout and stagnation, or, after they've gained some experience, some teachers transfer to affluent school districts where the issues are not as severe.

Second, many teachers have low morale due to the lack of support they receive from the school's administration. Many principals are not as responsive to the needs of teachers as they should be, nor do they provide teachers with clear and consistent feedback on their instructional practices. In a lot of urban schools, the principals are not accessible to teachers, and when they are available, they aren't privy to all the information necessary to render satisfactory decisions.

The reason for such inaccessibility and lack of support from the principal (or the school's administration as a whole) is mostly due to the principal's failure to work efficiently. These principals do not adhere to Laws 1, 6, and 9 discussed previously; therefore, they're tied up with issues and people that detract from the time that rightfully should be spent assisting teachers. Teachers look to the principal for leadership, and when they don't find it, it usually leaves them feeling alone, alienated, and unsure of themselves—especially if the teacher is relatively new to the profession.

I often compare the relationship between an urban school teacher and a principal to that of a prize fighter with a poor trainer. The trainer is supposed to give the fighter advice and correction in order to give the fighter the best chance at winning. Imagine what would happen if the fighter returned to his corner after each round and the trainer wasn't there to give advice, or if he was there, bad advice was given because he hadn't spent enough time with his fighter to know his strengths and weaknesses relative to the opponent.

Such a situation is detrimental not only to a fighter's career, but also to his health. The fighter will continue on out of sheer desire and a will to win, but may take an unnecessary beating in the process. After a few rounds, the fighter's eyes are swollen. A few more rounds, his nose is bloody and his lips are busted—making it hard to breathe. A few more rounds and the fighter's jaw is broken. Sooner or later, the fighter will be knocked completely out.

The same holds true for urban school teachers. Out of sheer passion and a strong desire to help students succeed, they go into the classroom and try to do the best they can. But within a short time, they experience things that they're unprepared to deal with—issues that were not taught to them in their undergraduate or graduate teaching programs.

When they turn to their principals for assistance, they often do not receive the support or advice needed to cope with their issues. So they take hit after unnecessary hit. Sooner or later two things usually happen: they take flight (resign, leave the profession, or transfer to an affluent school district with better working conditions) or they give up and quit (burn out, become stale, lose passion, stop trying to get better, become terminated, etc.). Some teachers are able to weather the storm and improve by means of their own raw talent or individual resilience, but those types are few and far between.

Last, but definitely not least, teachers lose morale due to increased student discipline problems. Student discipline takes on an entirely different meaning when speaking of inner-city schools. The behaviors are becoming increasingly more severe and out of control. Teachers in today's urban school classrooms are now being asked to deal with more student discipline issues within the classroom—many of which used to be issues handled by the school's administration.

As a result, teachers face more profane language, disrespect, and threats from students. Because many urban school teachers are unequipped to handle such issues, they resort to sending students out of class—usually to the principal's office. In many instances, the misbehaving student is sent back to class without any follow-up from the administration, creating a revolving cycle of students being sent back and forth from the classroom to the principal's office. This contributes to the teacher's frustration and drives them further toward the land of burnout, stagnation, frustration, and low self-efficacy.

STUDENT DISCIPLINE: WHY IS IT A PROBLEM FOR URBAN SCHOOLS?

In order to properly answer this question, we must first get to the root of the problem. Students who attend inner-city schools are not inherently unruly, nor are all inner-city school officials inadequate at handling student discipline issues. Discipline within urban schools is a huge issue because there are some factors that many principals fail to take under consideration.

For example, many of the communities where urban schools are located are plagued by a culture of violence, a history of unemployment, and generational poverty. These factors, combined with students who may be lacking one or more of their basic needs, creates a very interesting dynamic for teachers to deal with inside the classroom. Also, many teachers who work in urban/inner-city schools were not raised in the same environmental conditions as their students, nor do they live in the communities where they work.

This creates a huge disconnect between the teacher and the students they serve. A teacher's lack of understanding about the students' community dynamics and environmental background, can easily lead to increased behavioral problems in the classroom. The same holds true for the principal. This is why Law 2 (Learn the Culture of the School and Community) discussed previously is so important.

Another factor, and probably the most important, is the breakdown of the family unit within the majority of inner-city neighborhoods. Most of the households located within inner-city neighborhoods are headed by single women with usually more than one child—the biological mother or often the maternal grandmother.

Many of the social skills and behavioral values that would have been taught in the home are being replaced by values necessary for survival in the communities where they live—which usually doesn't mesh with behaviors needed to be successful in school. The attitudes students bring to school from their home environment, mixed with an unprepared teacher and a nonresponsive administrator, lead to a school with an abundance of student discipline issues.

There are a lot of single parents who head their households and do an outstanding job with their children—some have children who go on to do wonderful things. The problem is that when these children mingle in a school environment that's not conducive to learning, some of these students have a natural tendency to behave in ways that are similar to the dominant school environment. This is why a positive school culture must be established in every classroom, and throughout the school as a whole.

WHAT SHOULD PRINCIPALS DO?

Principals should adhere to Law 12 by developing a strategic plan for tackling both issues. Laws 2, 7, and 11 will assist toward the development of such a plan. Principals who are successful in implementing this law will be able to catapult their schools into new heights. Strategic planning should be a group process. Principals should not try to construct planning of this magnitude alone. They should solicit help from various stakeholders in order to get their opinions and suggestions.

When dealing with improving teacher morale, the primary goal of the plan should be to make teachers feel more appreciated, and to provide them with better means of support. Teachers who know they're being backed by the principal will feel more confident when dealing with tough issues. They will not feel neglected or unappreciated because they will be getting support on a consistent basis.

A strategic plan for student discipline is a matter of sending a clear and consistent message to all stakeholders involved (teachers, students, parents, etc.). First, the principal has to declare what is acceptable and unacceptable student behavior. This means providing clear oral and written communication that describes the behavioral expectations. Clearly communicating behavioral expectations could include, but is not limited to, using the district's code of conduct, adding policies in student handbooks, hanging wall postings in the halls, conducting informational sessions with parents and other stakeholders about student behavior, outlining information in the school's newsletter, explaining policies in letters to parents, and creating opportunities to review behavioral goals and expectations with students.

Next, develop consequences to reinforce the accepted behavior. Consequences should be progressive for each infraction (i.e., verbal warning, notify parent, assign detention, schedule a parent conference, and/or suspension). Every school district has a code of conduct for students that outlines possible consequences for various infractions. Principals should make sure that the consequences outlined to students and others are aligned with the district's student code of conduct. The consequences should also be shared with students and parents.

Third, the school's administration must be consistent with reinforcing the consequences. You can't be stern at the beginning of the year, and then slack off after a few months. Teachers must also be consistent with regard to how they handle disciplinary issues within the classroom. The expectations and consequences should also be used to help teachers design rules to govern their individual classes.

Most important, there should be a set of rewards for students who display acceptable behaviors. A school-wide strategic behavioral plan shouldn't be all punitive. The most attention should be given to students who are displaying proper behaviors, instead of giving negative attention to students who are misbehaving. This adds to creating a positive school culture.

Final note: the behavioral plan should be school-wide to promote consistency. It should be something that's sewn into the fabric of the school's culture and reinforced daily; therefore, stakeholders should be provided opportunities to contribute to the creation of such plans so that when these are unveiled to the greater community, they will be accepted and implemented by all.

EXAMPLE

"It literally took us three years to get this school under control, but we did it," stated Mr. Gilbert, principal of an inner-city school of 850 students. "The school was so out of hand, mainly due to a lack of consistent leadership. In the six years before I arrived, the school had five different principals and six different assistant principals. This led to disorganization.

"Students did whatever they wanted. They didn't follow the bell schedule, cut class by going to the gym and other places, left campus without permission, and some students even had keys to the main office and the elevator. The first thing I had to do was establish order and consistency. I closed access to certain doors for students, restricting students' ability to leave campus. I hired extra security and instituted hall sweeps for students who refused to go to class on time. After three infractions, students were given various consequences. Excessive hall walkers were suspended and were not allowed to return until a parent returned with them."

When asked how he was able to curb incidents of fighting among students, Gilbert responded, "We discovered that most of the fights that took place on school grounds were due to situations that took place in the surrounding neighborhoods. For some reason, students would wait to duke it out at school.

"We took a tough stance on fighting. Any student who engaged in fighting received a minimum of ten days of out-of-school suspension for the first offense, followed by a parent conference. Upon returning to school from suspension, we would have the parent, and student, sign a behavioral contract outlining proper behavior and what to do if the student should need assistance from an adult with any issue in the future.

"So, if a student engaged in another fight, he/she was suspended for ten more days with a recommendation for expulsion. Within a short time, parents began to take more of an active role in helping their children look for other ways to solve problems. We had similar processes for profanity toward staff, smoking, weapons, drugs, alcohol, and theft. We really had to send a tough message to everyone that those things were no longer tolerated in the school."

Essential Questions: Was the law followed in the above scenario? Why or why not? If yes, what actions did the principal take to adhere to the law? If not, what should the principal have done in order to have been more effective? What did you learn from the scenario? Would you do anything differently?

Conclusion

One of the most important questions facing educators today is, "How do we help students of low socioeconomic status achieve at the same levels as their affluent counterparts?" Many people believe that the way to improve education for this student population is by putting an effective teacher in every classroom. While there is a lot to be said about teacher effectiveness, I believe that school leadership effectiveness is just as, or more, important.

Principals play a major role in every aspect of school operations and functioning. They must juggle many tasks and duties, while serving the needs of a multitude of stakeholders. If the leaders are not properly prepared and equipped to handle the extremely tough circumstances that come with the position, then urban schools will continue to perform dismally and remain at the bottom of the nation in achievement.

Many politicians, educators, and scholars are now debating the state of public education in this country, and what it will take to make it work for all students. Students and families of low socioeconomic status rest at the center of this debate. It is my belief that every principal working in an urban school has a choice to either maintain the status quo, or actively work to bring about effective changes that will make urban schools work for urban communities. My hope is that after reading this book, urban school principals will be more prepared, ready, and armed with the knowledge they need in order to make true reform a reality, and not just something people talk about.

Being a principal of an urban school is very challenging, but it is also rewarding. If you are currently working as an administrator in an urban district, I applaud you. If you are still considering it, I hope you will decide to do so. In most cases, you will be serving a segment of America's youth that are underserved. You can take satisfaction in knowing you will be working with students for whom you can have the most positive impact. Urban youth deserve a chance at a quality education. Principals are the people who help to make it a reality.

The 12 laws discussed in this book contain intimate knowledge germane to the inner workings, problems, and people existing within the urban school setting. School leaders can take this information and use it to transform failing schools into places where learning flourishes. I've personally incorporated them in my own professional practice, and have experienced outstanding results. I'm sure you will experience the same.

THE BEST OF THE REST

As I stated in the preface of this book, the origin of the 12 laws came from interviews conducted during a qualitative case study I did years ago while in graduate school. While this particular book focuses on 12 of the most pertinent topics linked to urban school leadership, there are definitely other topics and issues to consider. Other topics that arose from my experience with the participants in the case study were also formulated into school leadership laws, but didn't make the cut for the final draft of this book. I call the laws that didn't make it "the best of the rest."

Even though the remaining laws didn't make the final cut after revisions, they're still very vital for the urban school principal's success, and play a major role in the overall success of urban schools as related to servicing students and the community at large. What follows is a brief discussion of these laws. I cover these issues, and many others, in more detail in my next book, *The Hard Truth: Problems Effecting Urban School Reform.* I hope that you will find the "best of the rest" as edifying as the 12 laws discussed previously.

Work Collaboratively with the School's PTA

It will serve the principal well to work collaboratively with the school's PTA. Many urban school principals and PTA representatives have an adversarial relationship. A lot of PTA members view the principal as being uncooperative, detached, and unresponsive to the issues that matter to them. Many urban school principals view PTA members as being combative, meddlesome, and more focused on the problems instead of helping to find solutions.

There are a lot of factors that contribute to this dysfunctional relationship, many of which are based on a particular school's circumstances, but the two groups must work together in order for the school to reach its maximum potential and for students to receive the best education possible. Because the principal is the school's leader, much of the responsibility for repairing the relationship lies with him/her.

Just as the school is an extension of the community, students are an extension of their parents. Schools can't rightfully expect to educate a child properly without including the parents and making them a necessary part of the equation. Urban school principals that are able to strengthen their relationships with their school's PTA are usually able to accomplish things more quickly, with less friction and turmoil.

Building and maintaining relationships with the PTA also closes the distance that often exists between urban schools and the communities where students live, creates a more inclusive school culture and community, and increases support for the school and its programs.

Be Cordial to Central Office Staff

It is no secret that a lot of principals in urban schools have issues and complaints about central office staff. The complaints are unique to each principal and each individual school setting, but the following are a few of the more common complaints:

- Too many people from central office are trying to tell principals how to run their schools; most have never served as principal, nor do they supervise building principals.
- Central office personnel are too far removed from what actually goes on in urban schools, and from the actual responsibilities of the principal.
- Central office personnel push too much unnecessary paperwork and mandates on principals.
- The people in central office never take the time to find out what principals in urban schools really need or desire before making decisions that will affect the way principals are able to operate their schools.
- Principals need more control and authority than some people in central office will relinquish. Principals need freedom and autonomy to operate their schools effectively.

Despite the above complaints, and others that are not listed, principals still need to be cordial to central office employees and work to build solid relationships with them as they would any other stakeholder. Of course there are obvious reasons why the two groups should get along with each other: both groups are employed by the same school district, and should work together on the common goal of educating students.

It is more advantageous for the principal to form a good relationship with central office employees because in some urban school districts, especially those with over 30,000 students, many central office personnel will never get to know anything about certain schools or the principals who run them, aside from what they read on paper or from what others in central office have to say. If a principal acts rude, disrespectful, and/or uncooperative to them, those messages will be spread to others in central office and could have an adverse impact on the school or the principal.

There are people in central office who have less powerful positions in relation to building-level principals, but these people serve those that are in higher positions. These people also often have the ear of those who can make life easier or more difficult for principals.

There are principals who always get the best resources and support, and receive timely information for the benefit of the school. These principals have no problems with making things happen for their schools. On the other hand, there are other principals who never receive (or they're last in line to get) needed support and resources for their schools. For example, they can never figure out why their documents never make it off someone's desk for processing. They wonder why they always experience delays and derailments.

Part of the reason why the unsuccessful principals are in such bad shape is because they haven't made an effort to build solid relationships with central office staff. In some extreme cases, the bonds principals form with central office staff not only make the difference with getting things processed more quickly, but in some extreme cases it could mean the difference between the principal being unemployed or not.

Seek Control of Your School's Budget

Most people in society are unaware of the enormous amount of money it takes to run a successful school district. Even those working in education often take the resources available to them for granted (e.g., technology, furniture, equipment, and/or human capital). The reality is that every pencil, chair, window blind, computer, chalkboard, desk, paper clip, copier, paper towel, or roll of bathroom tissue was once a line item on someone's budget.

All programs, personnel, and the overall vibrancy of the school rest with the school's budget. So it is imperative that urban school principals work to gain total control of their school's budget. As the school's leader, you should know more about what the school needs more than anyone else. Urban school principals should have a keen understanding of all program and personnel needs, and how much or little is needed for each to work effectively. Principals should have the autonomy to apply the school's financial resources in the most appropriate manner.

The problem is that most urban school districts have removed this power from the principal's hands. In some districts, school budget allocations are done from the central office level, while in other urban districts committees are set up to oversee the principal's budget decisions and the committee's approval is required before the principal can move forward.

These measures were put in place in a lot of urban schools for several reasons: some principals have historically abused this power, made poor financial decisions, or behaved unethically. In trying to minimize the damage from incompetent or neglectful principals, the people who instituted these restrictions created another problem—split decision making.

In most cases, the individuals who have the most control over the school's budget have overstepped their boundaries, and have inserted themselves in areas where they shouldn't be. In some extreme cases, they have ventured into curriculum and personnel issues. Split decision making is the fastest way to render a principal ineffective, and leave a school submerged in mediocrity or failure. Schools and principals find themselves in such a position because it is hard for all parties to form a consensus on the important issues when everyone is lobbying to use the budget for his/her own interest, and not the greater interest of the entire school.

Principals are the ones being held accountable for the school's success or failure, so they should rightfully have the most control. I'm not advocating that urban school principals shouldn't listen to the advice of other stakeholders, or shouldn't allow others in the decision-making process, but I am saying that principals should be given the final say as to how all funds should be spent.

In order for principals to be effective in their positions, they must seek to gain as much control over their schools' budgets as possible. If a principal is in a district where most of the decisions are made from central office, then the principal must actively work to become familiar with those making the decisions, and become part of the decision-making process. If a principal is working in a district where he/she has to get approval from a committee, then the principal must actively work to persuade the committee members to vote according to his/her ideas.

Build Partnerships with the Business Sector

Due to increasing budget shortfalls, tax abatements, and failed levies, many urban schools are lacking many of the resources needed to deliver the best education to students. The financial crunch can be felt in every aspect of school operations, from personnel to textbooks and materials.

One of the best ways principals can alleviate some of the burdens is by forming partnerships with members of the business sector. A school-business partnership is defined as a mutual agreement between a business and a school to establish certain goals and to construct a reasonable means of achieving those goals.

Forming a strong business partnership can help ease some financial pressure by not allowing schools to rely so heavily on public funds to support every educational program. It will also give members of the business community greater involvement with students and school programming. Businesses are often in positions to provide instructional materials and to support professional development for teachers. They may also be able to leverage additional resources that normally might not be available to school districts.

Urban school principals can't sit around and wait for more money and resources to come, because the reality is that more resources will not be coming. Principals need to become more assertive and actively look for alternative ways to make ends meet. Developing school-business partnerships is one of the best ways to do so.

Keep Your Office and Custodial Staff Happy

When a school's personnel is mentioned, the first employees that come to mind are teachers and principals. Those who truly know the inner workings of a school know that a school operates by means of a multitude of employees, not just teachers and principals. Some of the most valuable employees of a school are the office and custodial staff. It is to the principal's advantage to treat these employees well, and to establish a bond of mutual respect.

What I mean by a bond of mutual respect is that principals should show these employees how much they are appreciated, and let them know how valuable their job responsibilities are to the school. Many people underestimate the significance of a school's support staff, but principals shouldn't make such a mistake. The cleanliness of the school building and the temperament of the office are the first things that people notice when they visit the school. If the front office and the building's maintenance isn't in order, then people will make unfavorable judgments about the school before they even meet the principal, which could have negative consequences.

For example, parents do not want to send their children to a poorly maintained school building, nor will students be enthused to come. If parents choose other options for their children (private school, home school, etc.) then the school losing the students will lose funding, which could result in layoffs and in some extreme cases, school closings.

If students are the lifeblood of a school, then the support staff are the vital organs. Principals will do well in making sure these employees are happy.

Take Advantage of Social Media

We now live in a world where information is being transmitted and broadcast within seconds. People are using various outlets (Facebook, Twitter, You-Tube, MySpace, etc.) to communicate and stay connected with each other. Even the business sector has gravitated to this phenomenon, using social media to stay in tune with their customer base.

Urban schools shouldn't be the exception—they should also use social media to connect with their customer base as well. The base that urban schools need to be connected with is the community where students live. Utilizing social networks will help to close the distance that often exists between urban schools and the community. It will also help schools to dispense accurate information to community members regarding school events, programs, and incidents.

Social media outlets are also a great means for the community to communicate with the school. This way school officials can stay abreast of what's going on in the community, making both parties well informed. Many times, urban schools are behind the curve when it comes to implementing technology and trends that the greater society has embraced. This is why urban school principals need to be proactive, and constantly seek ways to use new technology for the betterment of their schools.

References

Angelica, E. (2001). *Crafting Effective Mission and Vision Statements*. St. Paul, MN: The Wilder Foundation.

Barth, R. (1990). *Improving Schools from Within*. San Francisco: Jossey-Bass.

Buffum, A., and Hinman, C. (2006). Professional learning communities: Reigniting passion and purpose. *Leadership*, 35(5), 16–19.

Daresh, J. (2006). *Beginning the Principalship: A Practical Guide for New School Leaders*. Thousand Oaks, CA: Corwin Press.

Erb, T. O., and Stevenson, C. (1999). From faith to facts: Turning points in action—What difference does teaming make? *Middle School Journal*, 30(3), 47–50.

Marzano, R. (2003). *What Works in Schools: Translating Research into Action*. Alexandria, VA: Association for Supervision and Curriculum Development.

Patterson, K., Grenny, J., McMillan, R., and Switzler, A. (2002). *Crucial Conversations: Tools for Talking When Stakes are High*. New York: McGraw Hill.

Payne, R. (2005). *A Framework for Understanding Poverty*. Highlands, TX: Aha! Process, Inc.

Reeves, D. (2002). *The Daily Disciplines of Leadership*. San Francisco: Jossey-Bass.

Robbins, P., and Alvy, H. (2003). *The Principal's Companion: Strategies and Hints to Make the Job Easier*. Thousand Oaks, CA: Corwin Press.

Sergiovanni, T. (1999). *Building Community in Schools*. San Francisco: Jossey-Bass.

Seyfarth, J. (1999). *The Principal: New Leadership for New Challenges*. Upper Saddle River, NJ: Prentice Hall.

Wiles, J., and Bondi, J. (1998). *Curriculum Development: A Guide to Practice*. Upper Saddle River, NJ: Prentice Hall.

Young, P. (2004). *You Have to Go to School—You're the Principal!: 101 Tips to Make It Better for Your Students, Your Staff, and Yourself*. Thousand Oaks, CA: Corwin Press.

About the Author

Sean B. Yisrael began his career as a high school social studies teacher; where he worked in an urban school district for seven years. In 2004, he moved into school administration—holding positions in school districts located in Ohio and Washington, DC. In 2010, Dr. Yisrael formed Educational Practitioners for Better Schools, a professional development company designed to provide low-cost professional development services for school districts who have trouble providing quality training for teachers, administrators, and parents. Dr. Yisrael is a lecturer, scholar, and an author; but most importantly he is an educator who is passionate about delivering a high quality education to students. Dr. Yisrael is the author of *12 Laws of Urban School Leadership: A Principal's Guide for Initiating Effective Change* (2012) and *Classroom Management: A Guide for Urban School Teachers* (2012), both published by Rowman & Littlefield Education.